Harper's Illustrated Handbook of Cats

A Chanticleer Press Edition

Harper's Illustrated Handbook of Cats

Health Care Section
by Robert W. Kirk, DVM

Edited by Roger Caras

With photographs by Richard J. Katris
and Nancy Katris

HarperPerennial

A Division of HarperCollins*Publishers*

For information address HarperCollins, Publishers, Inc., 10 East 53rd Street, New York, N.Y. 10022.

Prepared and produced by Chanticleer Press, Inc., New York.

Designed by Massimo Vignelli.

Color reproductions by Nievergelt Repro AG, Zurich, Switzerland.
Printed and bound by Dai Nippon, Tokyo, Japan.
Typeset in Garamond by Dix Type Inc., Syracuse, New York.

Published July 1985
Sixth Printing, July 1993

Library of Congress Cataloging in Publication Data

Harper's illustrated handbook of cats.

Includes index.
1. Cats.   2. Cat breeds.   3. Cat breeds —Pictorial works.
ISBN 0-06-091199-9 (pbk.)
I. Caras, Roger A.   II. Harper & Row, Publishers.   III. Title: Illustrated handbook of cats.
SF442.H35   1985   636.8   85-1331
ISBN 0-06-273165-3 (pbk)

Contents

Contributors

Roger Caras
is general editor and wrote the essays
The Origin of the Domestic Cat and A
Special Relationship. He is special
correspondent for ABC News in the field
of pets, wildlife, and the environment,
and columnist for several national
publications. He has written over fifty
books, including *The Roger Caras Pet
Book* and *The Private Lives of Animals.*

Robert W. Kirk, DVM
wrote the section Health Care, reviewed
the Potential Health Problems for each
breed, and evaluated the seriousness of
common disorders for the Key to
Potential Health Problems. He is author
of *First Aid for Pets,* coauthor of *The
Handbook of Veterinary Procedures and
Emergency Treatment* and *Small Animal
Dermatology,* and editor of *Current
Veterinary Therapy.* Dr. Kirk is professor
of medicine and director of the
Veterinary Medical Teaching Hospital,
New York State College of Veterinary
Medicine, Cornell University, and has
been a veterinarian for forty years.

Richard and Nancy Katris
photographed the breeds illustrated
specially for this guide. Their work has
appeared in *The Book of the Cat* and *The
Compleat Cat,* as well as in the magazines
Cats, Cat World, and *Cats Magazine.*
They have photographed prize-winning
cats for many breeders, and their pictures
are featured in the *Cat Fanciers'
Association Yearbook.* The team has also
contributed to the Kal-Kan/Winn
Foundation calendar. The Katrises'
studio is Chanan Photography in Mira
Loma, California.

Marna S. Fogarty
reviewed all the manuscript and
photographs for this guide. She is editor-
in-chief of the *Cat Fanciers' Association
Yearbook* and the magazine *Cat Fanciers'
Almanac,* and author of *The Cat Yellow
Pages.* She and her husband have an

Abyssinian, an American Shorthair, and
a Shaded Silver Persian.

Richard H. Gebhardt
reviewed the manuscript. He is a well-
known international CFA judge and
breeder, former president and chairman
of the Cat Fanciers' Association, and is
currently a member of the CFA board of
directors. Mr. Gebhardt served as
consultant editor for *A Standard Guide to
Cat Breeds.* He is president of the Empire
Cat Club in New York City, and owns
the Blue Ribbon Grooming Shop in
Denville, New Jersey.

Joan Bernstein
wrote all of the section Shorthair Cats,
except for the Abyssinian breed account;
she also contributed the Tiffany account.
She breeds Tonkinese, Siamese, and
Colorpoint Shorthairs, is president of the
Tonkinese Breed Association, editor of
The Aqua Eye, and contributes regularly
to the *Cat Fanciers' Association Yearbook.*

Judy Brocato
contributed the essay Raising a Kitten.
She and her husband breed Himalayans
and Persians at their cattery South Paw
in Rome, Georgia.

Edna Field
wrote the essays Grooming and Routine
Care and Showing Your Cat, as well as
the breed accounts for the Abyssinian,
Himalayan and Kashmir, Persian, and
Somali. As a breeder, she has specialized
in Abyssinians, Persians, and American
Shorthairs. She has been a CFA judge for
over twenty years and has officiated in
Denmark, Sweden, Holland, Germany,
Italy, Japan, Australia, and New
Zealand, in addition to North America.
Mrs. Field is columnist for *Cat World
Magazine* and has contributed to the *Cat
Fanciers' Association Yearbook* and *The
Complete Cat Encyclopedia.*

Rosemary Kendrick
contributed the essays How to Select a

Suitable Breed, The Mating Instinct, and Problem Solving. Since 1972, she has bred and shown purebred Silver Tabby American Shorthairs at her Silver Myne Cattery in Madison, Wisconsin. She edits "The American Connection," a quarterly newsletter of the National American Shorthair Club, and has written articles about cats for various publications, including the *Cat Fanciers' Association Yearbook*.

Jeanie McPhee
wrote the essay Body Language and the section Longhair Cats, except for the Himalayan and Kashmir, Persian, Somali, and Tiffany breed accounts. She is former chairman of the CFA Judging Program, former CFA director-at-large, and is currently an all-breed judge. She has contributed to *A Handbook for Cat People* and the *Cat Fanciers' Association Yearbook*. Additionally, Mrs. McPhee breeds Persians, Exotic Shorthairs, Manx, and Siamese at her cattery CO-MC in Houston, Texas.

Barbara Naviaux
is author of the Color Glossary and the essay Understanding Color Genetics. She has studied breeding and color genetics, has a bachelor's degree in biology, and is employed as a medical laboratory technician. Best known for her Cameo and Smoke Persians, Mrs. Naviaux has operated her Rodabi Cattery in Shingle Springs, California, since 1958. She has published numerous articles on coat color inheritance and is currently writing a book on longhair cats. She is a regular contributor to the *Cat Fanciers' Association Yearbook*.

Preface

The gentle company of a cat is one of
life's great pleasures. A familiar rub
against your leg, a low, rumbling purr of
contentment, or a soft warm creature
curled in your lap—these are special
delights that only a cat can offer.
The enjoyment of owning a cat is
accessible to everyone; all it really
requires is time and a generous heart.
Young people and old, large families and
single people, experts and novices—all
are able to give a cat the attention and
care it requires, and to receive, in return,
affection and companionship.
Whether you are an experienced owner
with a dozen champions to your credit
or a newcomer in search of your first pet,
selecting a cat that is right for you is a
challenging and exciting experience. It
also requires careful thought, for the cat
that you take home with you now will be
your companion and your responsibility
for many years to come.
Presented here are photographs and full
descriptions of 108 cats and kittens—
every breed and variety recognized in
America. The accounts provide a clear
and detailed profile of each breed, from
its personality and appearance to its
suitability for a particular environment.
The history of every breed is discussed as
well, along with special hints for care
and a warning about any health problems
to which a certain breed may be
susceptible. The Color Glossary defines
over 100 colors and patterns.
This book will help you choose the cat
that is best suited to your style of living.
But whatever cat you select, whether a
breed included here or a stray kitten
from the neighborhood, you will find
hours of pleasure browsing through
these pages.

How to Use This Guide

Whether you are looking for a breed to buy, already have a pet, or simply love cats, this book offers a new and fuller understanding of those wonderful companions—cats.

If You Are Trying to Choose a Pet

Are you thinking of buying your first cat? You will find that the lively color portraits of every breed recognized in America are particularly helpful. All of the cats pictured were photographed specially for this book, and many are show champions. The essays on choosing the right cat give tips on what to look for and evaluate the special appeal of a longhair or shorthair cat. The Key to Breed Characteristics provides a quick evaluation of each breed, rating its suitability for children or as a companion, its playfulness and talkativeness, as well as how much grooming time is required. Raising a Kitten offers advice for the early, often difficult, weeks of adjustment; and Grooming and Routine Care provides hints on everyday requirements.

If a Cat Walks into Your Life

Has a lost cat suddenly arrived at your door? You will find guidelines on feeding, bedding, vaccinations, and even emergency first-aid treatment in the Health Care section. By looking through the color plates, you will be able to identify a purebred or find clues leading to a stray's purebred relatives—no matter how remote.

If You Are an Experienced Cat Owner

As a cat owner, you can discover more about your favorite breeds, learn about the origin of the cat as a companion, and trace the history of both longhair and shorthair breeds in the cat fancy. If you are considering breeding your cat, read The Mating Instinct. Is your pet scratching your furniture? Consult the essay Problem Solving for practical solutions. Perhaps you are considering the show ring; Showing Your Cat offers pointers on how to prepare for a cat show.

If You Can't Have Your Own Cat

Have you always loved cats but never been able to own one? You will be captivated by the striking photographs of America's finest purebreds and intrigued by the penetrating insights into their personalities. The essay Body Language analyzes the subtle meaning behind the flick of a tail or the twitching of the ears. Here you will find all kinds of fascinating cat lore. The American Shorthair—one of our first breeds—has roamed these shores since the Pilgrims first landed in Massachusetts. The Birman is said to have been held in such high esteem by the Kittaha monks of Burma that the theft of a cat was considered a sacrilege.

While not all breeds have an exalted or mysterious history, each cat has its own particular appeal. In these pages you will discover many beguiling and beautiful creatures—each of them promising a lifetime of friendship.

The Cat's Anatomy

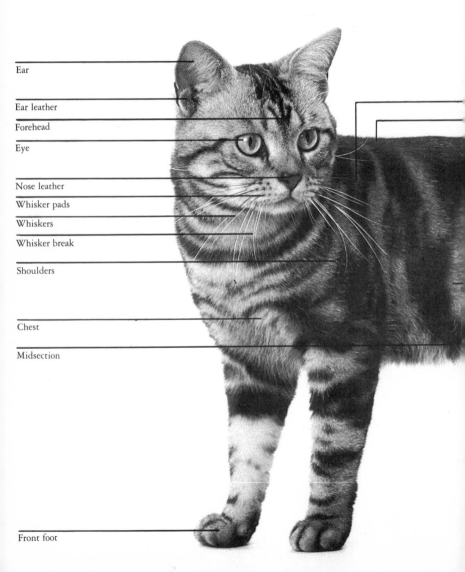

Ear

Ear leather

Forehead

Eye

Nose leather

Whisker pads

Whiskers

Whisker break

Shoulders

Chest

Midsection

Front foot

Ear tuft

Nose break

Cheek

Mask

Muzzle

Jowls

Chin

Bib

Neck

Shoulder blades

Back

Rump

Base of tail

Tail

Torso

Flank

Thigh

Hock

Back foot

Paw pads

The Origin of the Domestic Cat

Wild Ancestors

Rooted in the ancient past, theories about the origin of the domestic cat are part fact and inevitably part speculation. But as far as we know, cats were first tamed in Egypt, probably around 1600 B.C. or slightly before, coinciding with the invention of the silo for storing grain. Stored grain attracts rats and mice, vermin that we know today's cats find attractive. In ancient Egypt and the rest of North Africa, it was a species of small wild cat, *Felis libyca,* in which the silo keepers would have observed this trait; presumably these same silo keepers were the first to harness this innate feline talent by officially employing cats as ratters and mousers. (Some believe that the North African wild cat is a subspecies of the European wild cat, *Felis sylvestris,* which would give it the scientific name *Felis sylvestris libyca.* Other authorities consider *F. libyca* and *F. sylvestris* simply different geographic races of the same species.)

Undoubtedly the Egyptians captured some adult wild cats, but probably had far better luck with kittens, which they were able to find by tracking adults back to their dens. If taken as adults, all species of wild cats are characteristically ferocious and unmanageable. They virtually never settle down or accept any familiarity. Very young wild cats, however, can frequently be socialized with gentle and patient handling.

Selective Breeding

Once the ancient silo keepers had tamed some of the wild cats, they could start the real process of domestication: selective breeding. It is doubtful that the ancient people of Egypt understood genetics. How they were able to breed desirable characteristics into their animals remains a mystery. The same mystery surrounds the origin of the domestic dog thousands of years earlier. But somehow, from the wild cat of North Africa they began shaping an entirely new species, *Felis catus,* our modern domestic cat.

Today in the United States there are fewer than forty breeds of the domestic cat, less than ten percent of the worldwide number of dog breeds. Compared with dogs, cats are much less flexible genetically. In terms of size and weight alone, for instance, dogs are much more diverse, ranging from the smallest at two to three pounds to the largest at two hundred thirty pounds or more. But new cat breeds are constantly being shaped, just as they have been for nearly four thousand years into the forms that exist today, varieties or breeds that please us, satisfy aesthetic ideals and our fickle tastes.

Though of less economic importance than the horse, dog, sheep, cow, or other animals man has ever domesticated or extracted from the wild, the cat has served us faithfully for millennia, not just as a ratter and mouser, but as a companion with qualities unequaled in any other species. The ancient Egyptians launched a wonder that lives on with us to this very day.

A Special Relationship

Long-standing Ties

Between people and cats there exists a bond that has endured some four thousand years, an emotional tie with all kinds of aesthetic and intellectual overtones. This relationship, based on much more than mere convenience, is no easy thing to define. Cats have always had a positive influence on the lives of the vast number of people who keep them, and people are keeping them now in record numbers. As evidence of the domestic feline's status among us today, more books about cats are being published than ever before.

Aesthetic Appeal

Cats are beautiful. They appeal to our aesthetic sense, and this is obvious in art and literature, where they have forever been fixtures. Judging from the number of cats that appear in paintings by masters who recorded the lives of royalty, cats must have adorned palaces and courts in every land. They have been depicted by the greatest artists of every era in so many cultures that we cannot doubt that most people, clearly people of discernment, have thought them beautiful to look at. And in literature— where does the cat *not* appear? Think of Colette, or T. S. Eliot. Here the most accomplished and sensitive people among us have written that the cat is a special animal with extraordinary powers to please and delight. Cats sat in the laps of popes and were painted there, they played with the children of kings and were recorded there. The ancient Egyptians, who first domesticated the feline, esteemed cats so highly that they deified them and would kill anyone who caused them harm. Purebred or stray, in laps of luxury or of poverty, cats enjoy a universal appeal.

Emotional Interaction

Cats are dependent on us. It is true that no domesticated breed or variety is so lacking in the basic instincts of the ancestral wild cat that, if turned loose to become feral, it can't stalk, hunt, and kill what it needs to survive. But the cats we keep are not required to sustain themselves as hunters returned to the wild. As domestic creatures, they demand affection and attention. We coddle them, baby them, and figure out how to please them more, sometimes more than we try to please other people. Why? Simply because they are superb at returning love in kind.

Those who least understand cats proclaim them aloof, independent, opportunistic. Yet it hardly seems possible than an animal with those characteristics could be the center of so much attention. More often than not cats take their lead from us in a relationship. A cat treated tenderly, cared for well, and invited to sit in your lap or by your side will prove that no warmer friend can be found. But if you are indifferent, a cat is doubly so. If you are rough or cold, it is under the bed or looking the other way. Cats vary in their responses to human emotions, just as people vary in the feelings they project to one another. Just as there is no one cat, there is no one style or level of interaction between a cat and a person. The relationship is as rich as we want it to be. In the centuries that have passed since man first took the cat on as a companion and a helpmate, the evidence shows only that the relationship has been mutually rewarding.

How to Select a Suitable Breed

Choosing a Compatible Pet

Many people are enchanted by a stray cat or kitten that camps on their doorstep, a sweet face in the pet-store window, or longing eyes peering from a humane-society cage. The match may work out wonderfully over the years—but then again, it may not. Purebred and mixed-breed cats come in such a wide variety of types and temperaments that it is unrealistic to expect every cat to suit every person. Owner and pet may coexist happily for years yet never achieve that special closeness enjoyed by true kindred spirits. It is worth taking some time to do your homework: Get to know the individual cat in order to acquire the perfect pet for you.

Above all, do not make a spur-of-the-moment decision just because a kitten is cute. Remember that all kittens are cute, and even most adult cats are lovely and graceful. Think about how the kitten will behave, and how it will interact with you and with your children.

Each individual cat has its own personality. Beyond that, cat breeds have distinctive temperaments, as do bloodlines within breeds. Research the different breeds before starting your search. Read the breed accounts in this book carefully, then talk to cat owners, and visit breeders. The local cat club is an excellent way to get information about various breeds; your veterinarian can probably put you in touch with club leaders. Look for a cat show in your area that you can attend; the cat show presents a wonderful opportunity to see many different kinds of cats.

An Appealing Appearance

Probably most people's first consideration is how the animal looks. Cats come in an assortment of sizes, shapes, and colors. Do you prefer a large, solid animal like a Persian or an American Shorthair, or a delicate little cat like a Siamese or a Cornish Rex? A big, round head or a long, pointed head? Remember that you will be looking at that face for years to come. Do the warm colors—reds, creams, browns—appeal to you, or do you prefer a cool silver or blue? Do you like the dramatic markings of a calico or tabby, or do you want a solid color? Each person's taste is different, and there is no reason why people should not get exactly what they fancy the most.

One of the more important decisions when it comes to physical appearance is whether you want a longhair or shorthair cat. Some people love long flowing fur, whereas others want their pets to be sleek and shiny. There is more than just aesthetics involved in the decision; coat length makes a real difference in the amount of work required. Shorthair cats more or less keep themselves groomed. Longhair cats, on the other hand, need to be combed or brushed almost daily or they will leave clouds of fur around the house and develop tangles in their coat and hair balls in their stomach. This grooming must be done week after week, year after year, as long as the cat lives.

Temperament Testing

The last quality people usually consider is really the most important—temperament. You should not select a cat on physical appearance alone. The cat's personality will determine how successfully it shares your home and life-style and whether the two of you will ever really be compatible.

It is easier to evaluate temperament in a purebred than in a mixed-breed cat. First, you can read about the breed's characteristics. Then, in most cases, you can visit the breeder's home, discuss his or her breeding program, and see how the kittens are raised. This is crucial, because the amount and type of human handling in the first few weeks of life plays a large part in a kitten's permanent attitude toward people. You also should be able to see one or both parents and evaluate their dispositions, which tend to be passed along to offspring.

Judging a mixed-breed kitten is more difficult. With a stray, you will know nothing of its parents or early life. Pet shops also reveal little about their animals' backgrounds, and sometimes the kittens have had very little human contact. Humane societies usually can give you only sketchy information at best. People who advertise kittens "free to good home" in the newspaper often do not even know the cat that sired the litter.

If you want a mixed-breed, consider adopting an adult cat rather than a kitten. Almost all kittens are active and outgoing, but with an unknown background you are taking a chance that the kitten could grow up to be nervous, timid, aloof, or even aggressive. With an adult, on the other hand, temperament is already established and there for you to see. If you and the cat seem to hit it off, the animal should be able to adjust easily to your home.

What Is Your Ideal Cat?

Think carefully about your life-style before choosing a pet. Sit down and list the qualities that your ideal pet would have. Then look for that ideal pet. In general, if you want an active cat, think in terms of a shorthair; if your ideal is a quiet, well-mannered cat, consider the longhairs.

For an elderly person, the gentle presence of a Persian or Himalayan might be far preferable to the noisy activity of a Siamese. A retired person might find the required daily grooming a pleasant way to pass the time. On the other hand, a busy, career-oriented couple probably would not want a cat that requires much extra care, and might do well with an independent, easygoing breed like the American Shorthair rather than a demanding cat like the Burmese, which may resent being left alone.

A family with young children should avoid a cat that is either high-strung or shy. A high-strung cat might strike out at the children during rough play; a shy cat might spend its time hiding under the bed, much to the children's frustration. Look for a calm, bold, friendly animal. If possible, let the children interact with it before you bring it home to see whether they like each other.

Older children can have marvelous fun with a smart, lively cat such as a Siamese, Abyssinian, or Somali; people say they can teach these cats to walk on leashes and shake hands. A homebound single person probably would enjoy a sensitive, eager-to-please cat such as the curly-coated Cornish Rex or the tailless Manx, both of which become extremely devoted to their owners. Those who entertain often might want an elegant, exotic cat they can proudly present to their friends. Many of the rarer breeds fit this description, including the svelte Oriental Shorthair, which resembles the Siamese yet comes in a wide array of stunning colors.

A final note about life-style: If you are away from home a great deal yet want a cat, why not consider getting two? That way the cats will have each other for companionship and are less likely to become destructive out of sheer boredom. Whatever type of cat you select, you will discover that given the care and love it needs, a cat can make a wonderful pet and devoted companion.

The Right Cat for You

Evaluating Your Choices

Choosing a pet is an important decision. Not only will your cat be a companion for years to come, but it will also become a member of your family. A pet is a pleasure and a responsibility. Its needs for proper care—from grooming to good nutrition and plenty of love—must be met in order to make it a welcome and happy member of your household. Not everyone, however, can devote the same amount of time to a cat; nor does everyone seek the same temperament, personality, or appearance in a breed.

A Key to Breed Characteristics

To help you select the right cat, the Key to Breed Characteristics establishes five categories, according to which every breed recognized in America is evaluated. These categories tell you if a cat is good with children, a good companion, playful, or talkative; it also tells how much grooming care is needed. For each category, a breed is rated high, moderate-to-high, moderate, moderate-to-low, or low. By definition, longhair cats require more grooming time than shorthair cats; thus, the rating for a longhair breed indicates more time than the same rating for a shorthair cat. On the chart, the breeds are divided into longhair cats and shorthair cats, just as they are divided in the color plates and the breed accounts.

Key to Breed Characteristics

	Good with Children	Good Companion	Playful	Talkative	Grooming Care
Longhair Cats					
Balinese	●	●	●	●	●
Birman	●	●	●	○	●
Cymric	●	●	●	●	●
Himalayan	●	●	○	○	●
Javanese	●	●	●	●	●
Kashmir	○	○	○	○	○
Maine Coon	●	●	●	○	●
Shorthair Cats					
Abyssinian	●	●	●	○	●
American Shorthair	●	●	●	●	●
American Wirehair	○	●	○	●	○
Bombay	●	●	●	○	●
British Shorthair	●	●	○	●	●
Burmese	●	●	●	○	●
Chartreux	●	●	○	●	●
Colorpoint Shorthair	●	●	●	●	●
Cornish Rex	●	●	●	○	○
Devon Rex	○	●	●	○	○
Egyptian Mau	○	○	○	●	●
Exotic Shorthair	●	○	○	●	○
Havana Brown	●	●	●	○	●

Color Key
- ● High
- ● Moderate-to-high
- ○ Moderate
- ● Moderate-to-low
- ● Low

	Good with Children	Good Companion	Playful	Talkative	Grooming Care
Norwegian Forest Cat	●	●	●	●	●
Persian	●	●	●	●	●
Ragdoll	●	●	●	●	●
Somali	●	●	●	●	●
Tiffany	●	●	●	●	●
Turkish Angora	●	●	●	●	●
Japanese Bobtail	●	●	●	●	●
Korat	●	●	●	●	●
Malayan	●	●	●	●	●
Manx	●	●	●	●	●
Ocicat	●	●	●	●	●
Oriental Shorthair	●	●	●	●	●
Russian Blue	●	●	●	●	●
Scottish Fold	●	●	●	●	●
Siamese	●	●	●	●	●
Singapura	●	●	●	●	●
Snowshoe	●	●	●	●	●
Sphynx	●	●	●	●	●
Tonkinese	●	●	●	●	●

Eye Colors

Beautiful, mysterious eyes are one of a cat's most beguiling features. Their color almost seems to change hue with the light. In some breeds, such as the Persian or American Shorthair, eye color is very important in judging show cats, but in other breeds, such as the Maine

Odd-eyed

Gold

Amber

Copper

Green

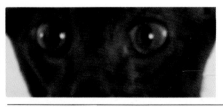

Vivid Green

Luminous Green

Green

Blue-green

Vivid Blue

Coon, any harmonious eye color is
acceptable. This table illustrates the
range of hues seen in cats' eyes.

Gold

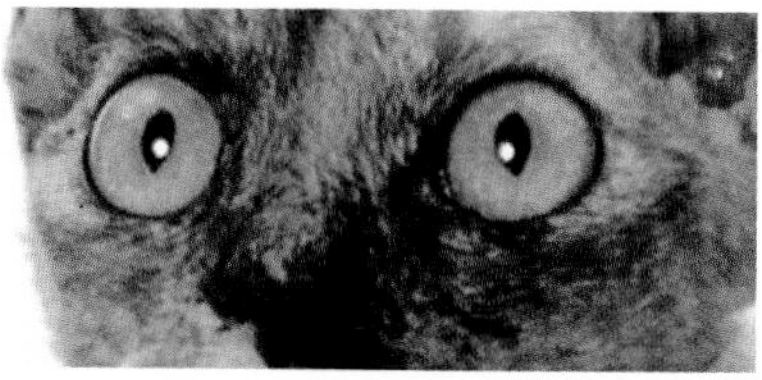

Gold

Copper

Copper

Gooseberry-green

Green

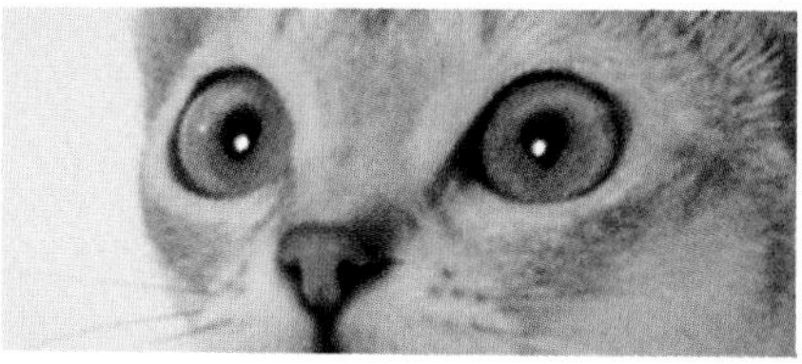

Green

Vivid Green

Blue

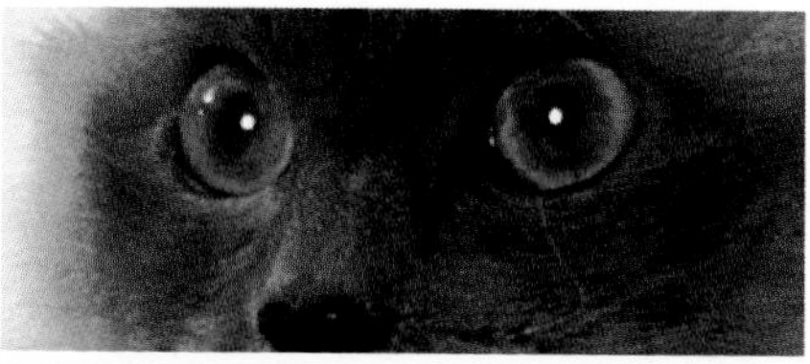

Blue

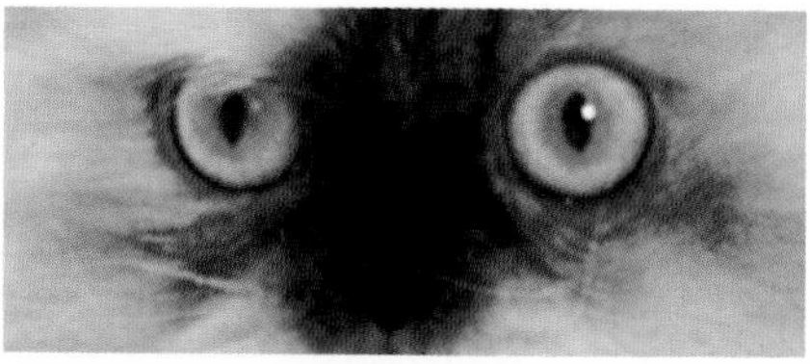

Colors and Patterns

The colors and patterns of cats are usually separated into five basic divisions: solid colors; particolors; shaded (tipped) colors; point restricted colors; and tabby patterns. To help familiarize you with this terminology, this table illustrates several examples of

Solid Colors	White	Red

Particolors	Blue and White	Black and White

Shaded (Tipped) Colors	Shaded Cameo	Shaded Silver

Point Restricted Colors	Seal Point	Lilac Point

Tabby, Ticked, and Spotted Patterns	Mackerel Tabby	Classic Tabby

each color division. In the Color
Glossary, the colors and patterns are
described according to the five divisions
illustrated here. Additionally, unique
breed colors are also described in a
separate part of the glossary.

Blue	Black	Chocolate	

Blue-Cream	Tortoiseshell	Calico	Van Calico

Black Smoke	Smoke Tortoiseshell		

Blue Point	Blue-Cream Point	Tortie Point	Seal-Lynx Point

Mackerel Tabby and White	Patched Tabby and White	Ticked	Spotted

Body Types

Purebred cats are often classified according to three body types: svelte, cobby, and intermediate build. At one extreme, the svelte or Oriental body type is lithe and fine-boned, with tapering lines and a narrow, wedge-shaped head. Svelte breeds appear very lightweight.

Svelte or Oriental Build

Siamese   Colorpoint Shorthair

Intermediate Build

Havana Brown   Burmese

Abyssinian   Somali

Birman   Maine Coon

Himalayan   Persian

Cobby Build

At the other extreme, the cobby body type is powerful, deep-chested, and large-boned, with a short, compact build low on the leg, and a large, rounded head. Cobby cats generally appear to be quite big. Most other cat builds are between these two extremes.

| Oriental Shorthair | Singapura | Balinese | Russian Blue |

| Tonkinese | Bombay | Egyptian Mau | Korat |

| American Wirehair | American Shorthair | Japanese Bobtail | Turkish Angora |

Scottish Fold

| Kashmir | Exotic Shorthair | British Shorthair |

1 Cymric

This white Cymric kitten is 12 weeks old. The coat is just beginning to develop. Like all young kittens, it has blue eyes.
Page 87.

3 Maine Coon

Red tabby Maine Coon kittens already have ear tufts and substantial bone structure. At 7 to 8 weeks the classic pattern is clearly defined. Their deep red markings will become even richer as they mature. These kittens are 10 weeks old.
Page 89.

2 Turkish Angora

A litter of 4 classic white Turkish Angora kittens shows the proper purity of color. Their nose leather and paw pads are pink. At 7 weeks their eyes are distinctly blue.
Page 96.

4 Persian

At 8 weeks these shaded silver kittens have mascara-outlined, blue-green eyes. Their paw pads are also black, but the nose leather is brick-red. The large, round eyes give these kittens their particularly sweet expression.
Page 91.

5 Tortie Point Himalayan

Cream-white to fawn body. Seal-brown mottled with red and/or cream on mask, ears, legs, feet, and tail. Red or cream facial blaze desirable. Nose leather and paw pads are seal, mottled with flesh-color and/or coral-pink. Blue eyes.
Page 88.

7 Blue-Cream Point Himalayan

Bluish-white or cream-white body shades gradually to white on chest and stomach. Patches of blue mixed with cream on mask, ears, legs, feet, and tail. Nose leather and paw pads may be slate-blue, pink, or mottled. Blue eyes.
Page 88.

6 Seal Point Himalayan

Fawn to cream body shades to lighter tone on chest and stomach. Dark seal-brown, almost black, on mask, ears, legs, feet, and tail. Nose leather and paw pads are seal. Blue eyes.
Page 88.

8 Blue Point Himalayan

Bluish-white body shades to white on chest and stomach. Blue on mask, ears, legs, feet, and tail. Nose leather and paw pads darker slate-blue. Blue eyes.
Page 88.

9 Flame Point Himalayan

Cream-white body with orange-flame to dark red on mask, ears, legs, feet, and tail. Nose leather and paw pads are flesh-color to coral-pink. Blue eyes.
Page 88.

11 Odd-eyed White Persian

Glistening white coat. Nose leather and paw pads are pink. The odd-eyed white Persian has a blue eye and a copper eye, each with equal depth of color and brilliance.
Page 91.

10 Shaded Cameo Persian

White undercoat with orange-red tipping. Darkest on top, shading to white on chin, chest, and undersides. Face and legs match. Nose leather, paw pads, and rims of eyes are rose. Copper eyes.
Page 91.

12 Shaded Silver Persian

White undercoat with delicate black tipping. Darkest on top, with white on chin, chest, and undersides. Face and legs match. Black outlines eyes, nose, and lips. Nose leather is brick-red. Paw pads are black. Green or blue-green eyes.
Page 91.

13 Van Calico Persian

White body with patches of red and black on face, legs, and tail. 1 or 2 small colored patches may appear on body. Nose leather and paw pads are usually pink. Copper eyes.
Page 91.

15 Red Persian

Deep, rich, brilliant red coat without any markings, shading, or ticking. Lips and chin are same red. Nose leather and paw pads are brick-red. Copper eyes.
Page 91.

14 Blue-Cream Persian

Blue with cream patches on body and extremities. Cream facial blaze desirable. Nose leather and paw pads may be blue, pink, or mottled. Copper eyes.
Page 91.

16 Red Classic Tabby Persian

Deep, rich red classic tabby markings on light red ground. Lips and chin are also red. Nose leather and paw pads are brick-red. Copper eyes.
Page 91.

17 Tortoiseshell Persian

Black ground with patches of red and cream on body and extremities. Red or cream facial blaze desirable. Nose leather and paw pads are generally black. Copper eyes.
Page 91.

19 Black Persian

Dense coal-black coat from roots to tips. Nose leather is black. Paw pads are black or brown. Copper eyes.
Page 91.

18 Brown Classic Tabby Persian

Dense black classic tabby markings on rich copper-brown ground. Matching lips, chin, and rings around eyes. Back of legs, from paw to heel, is black. Nose leather is brick-red. Paw pads are black or brown. Copper eyes.
Page 91.

20 Chocolate Kashmir

Solid, warm, rich chocolate-brown from roots to tips. Nose leather and paw pads are same brown. Copper eyes.
Page 88.

21 Tiffany

Always solid sable-brown from roots to tips. Nose leather and paw pads are brown to brownish pink. Gold eyes. Page 95.

23 Seal Point Birman

Warm, even, pale fawn to cream body shades gradually to lighter color on chest and stomach. Seal-brown on mask, ears, legs, and tail; white gloves. Nose leather matches points. Paw pads are pink. Blue to violet eyes.
Page 86.

22 Brown Classic Tabby Norwegian Forest Cat

Dense black classic tabby markings on rich copper-brown ground. Matching lips, chin, and rings around eyes. Back of legs, from paw to heel, is black. Nose leather is brick-red. Paw pads are black or brown. Green eyes.
Page 90.

24 Blue Point Birman

Bluish-white body shades almost to white on chest and stomach. Deep blue on mask, ears, legs, and tail; white gloves. Nose leather is slate-blue. Paw pads are pink. Blue to violet eyes.
Page 86.

25 Brown Mackerel Tabby and White Maine Coon

Dense black mackerel tabby markings on rich copper-brown ground. Bib, belly, and all 4 paws must be white. Black or brown nose leather and paw pads desirable, other colors acceptable. Green, gold, or copper eyes.
Page 89.

27 Blue-Cream Maine Coon

Blue with cream patches on body and extremities. Nose leather is brick-red. Paw pads are usually blue or mottled blue-cream; other colors also acceptable. Green, gold, or copper eyes.
Page 89.

26 Black Maine Coon

Dense coal-black coat from roots to tips. Nose leather is black. Paw pads are black or brown. Green, gold, or copper eyes. Page 89.

28 Calico Maine Coon

White with patches of black and red. White predominates on undersides and legs. Nose leather and paw pads are pink and/or black. Green, gold, or copper eyes. Page 89.

29 Ruddy Somali

Glowing orange-brown or ruddy color, ticked with black; darkest shading along spine. Entire underside is ruddy color. Nose leather is tile-red. Paw pads are black or brown. Gold or green eyes. Page 94.

31 Red Classic Tabby Cymric

Deep, rich red classic tabby markings on light red ground. Lips and chin are also red. Nose leather and paw pads are brick-red. Copper eyes. Page 87.

30 Red Somali

Deep, warm, glowing red with chocolate-brown ticking. Tips of ears and tail are same brown. Nose leather is rosy pink. Paw pads are pink with chocolate between toes. Gold or green eyes.
Page 94.

32 Red Mackerel Tabby Cymric

Light red ground with deep, rich red mackerel tabby markings. Lips and chin are red. Nose leather and paw pads are brick-red. Copper eyes.
Page 87.

33 Red-Lynx Point Javanese

Warm cream-white body with barred points. Deep red bars are separated by lighter ground. Ears are red with pale thumbprint. Nose leather and paw pads are flesh-color or coral. Vivid blue eyes. Page 85.

35 Lilac Point Balinese

Glacial white body. Mask, ears, legs, feet, and tail are frosty gray with pinkish tone. Nose leather and paw pads are lavender-pink. Vivid blue eyes. Page 85.

34 Seal-Lynx Point Javanese

Cream to pale fawn body shades to lighter undersides. Points have seal-brown bars separated by lighter ground. Ears are seal with light thumbprint. Nose leather is seal or seal edged with pink. Paw pads are seal. Vivid blue eyes. Page 85.

36 Chocolate Point Balinese

Ivory body with warm milk-chocolate on mask, ears, legs, feet, and tail. Nose leather and paw pads are cinnamon-pink. Vivid blue eyes. Page 85.

37 Mitted Seal Point Ragdoll

Fawn body with seal-brown on mask, ears, legs, and tail. White mittens. White stripe of varying width runs from bib, between forelegs, to under base of tail. Nose leather and paw pads are seal. Blue eyes.
Page 93.

39 Black and White Turkish Angora

Black and white with white on muzzle, chest, undersides, legs, and feet. An inverted "V" facial blaze desirable. Nose leather and paw pads are usually pink; black shown also acceptable. Amber eyes. This kitten is 10 to 12 weeks old.
Page 96.

38 Blue Turkish Angora

Lighter shade of blue is preferable to darker shade, but single, level tone from nose to tip of tail is most important. Nose leather and paw pads are blue. Amber eyes.
Page 96.

40 White Turkish Angora

Classic pure white with pink nose leather and paw pads. Eyes may be blue, amber, or one of each color.
Page 96.

41 Scottish Fold

At birth kittens do not have folded ears. Ears bend forward and downward at about 3 to 4 weeks or slightly later. The tabby kittens shown are 5 weeks old. Their eye color has not changed yet. Page 122.

43 Siamese

Siamese kittens are all white when born, gradually taking on color at the ears, nose, tail, and then the toes. The seal point kitten at left and the chocolate point kitten at right are 14 weeks old. Page 123.

42 Exotic Shorthair

The blue-cream kitten at left and the blue one at right are 8 weeks old. They already display this breed's characteristic plush coat, full cheeks, and shortened face.
Page 113.

44 Abyssinian

At birth kittens vary from dark orange with black patches to almost all black. Coat color and ticking develop slowly. Some kittens do not get full ticking until 6 months or older. The ruddy kittens shown are 7½ weeks old.
Page 101.

45 Red Abyssinian

Warm, glowing red coat with chocolate-brown ticking. Dark red tones preferred. Ears and tail have chocolate-brown tips. Nose leather is rosy pink. Paw pads are pink, with chocolate between toes and slightly beyond. Gold or green eyes.
Page 101.

47 Blue Abyssinian

Blue-gray coat ticked with slate-blue. Ivory undercoat. Creamy to beige undersides and forelegs. Slate-blue tail tip. Nose leather is dark pink. Paw pads are mauve, with slate-blue between toes. Gold or green eyes.
Page 101.

46 Ruddy Abyssinian

Ruddy brown coat with brown or black ticking. Rich orange-brown undercoat. Tail tipped with black. Nose leather is tile-red. Paw pads are black or brown, with black between toes and slightly beyond. Gold or green eyes.
Page 101.

48 Russian Blue

Bright, even blue, lighter shades preferred. Silver-tipped outer hairs create characteristic silvery sheen. Nose leather is slate-gray. Paw pads are lavender-pink or mauve. Green eyes.
Page 121.

49 Chartreux

Any shade of blue acceptable, as long as coat is same color from roots to tips.
Nose leather and paw pads are slate-blue.
Gold or copper eyes.
Page 108.

51 Burmese

Rich, warm, sable-brown coat shades imperceptibly to lighter undersides.
Nose leather and paw pads are brown.
Yellow to gold eyes.
Page 107.

50 Bombay

Fine, short, satiny black coat looks like patent leather. Nose leather and paw pads are black. Gold to copper eyes. Page 105.

52 Blue Malayan

Medium blue coat with warm fawn overtones. Color is slightly lighter on undersides. Nose leather and paw pads are slate-gray. Yellow to gold eyes. Page 117.

53 Champagne Malayan

Warm honey-beige coat shades to pale gold-tan on undersides. Color should be even but slight darkening allowed on face and ears. Nose leather is light, warm brown. Paw pads are warm pinkish tan. Yellow to gold eyes.
Page 117.

55 Blue Mink Tonkinese

Soft blue gray body with slate-blue on mask, ears, legs, feet, and tail. Body lighter hue underneath and may have fawn overtones. Nose leather and paw pads are slate-gray, sometimes with rose tinge. Blue-green eyes.
Page 127.

54 Platinum Malayan

Pale silvery-gray coat with pale fawn overtones, slightly lighter on undersides. Nose leather and paw pads are lavender-pink. Yellow to gold eyes.
Page 117.

56 Natural Mink Tonkinese

Medium brown body with dark brown on mask, ears, legs, feet, and tail. Body lighter hue underneath. Nose leather is dark brown. Paw pads are medium to dark brown, sometimes with rose tinge. Blue-green eyes.
Page 127.

57 Seal Point Siamese

Pale, even fawn to cream body gradually shades to lighter tone on chest and stomach. Deep seal-brown on mask, ears, legs, feet, and tail. Nose leather and paw pads are seal. Vivid blue eyes.
Page 123.

59 Lilac Point Siamese

Glacial white body with frosty gray, pink-tinged hue on mask, ears, legs, feet, and tail. Nose leather and paw pads are lavender-pink. Vivid blue eyes.
Page 123.

58 Chocolate Point Siamese

Ivory-colored body with warm milk-chocolate on mask, ears, legs, feet, and tail. Nose leather and paw pads are cinnamon-pink. Vivid blue eyes.
Page 123.

60 Blue Point Siamese

Bluish-white body gradually shades to white on chest and stomach. Deep blue on mask, ears, legs, feet, and tail. Nose leather and paw pads are slate. Vivid blue eyes.
Page 123.

61 Blue-Cream Point Colorpoint Shorthair

Bluish-white to platinum-gray body shades to lighter undersides. Points are deep blue-gray, mottled with cream. Facial blaze desirable. Nose leather and paw pads are slate, preferably mottled with flesh or coral-pink. Vivid blue eyes. Page 109.

63 Seal-Lynx Point Colorpoint Shorthair

Cream to pale fawn body shades to lighter undersides. Points have seal-brown bars separated by lighter ground. Ears are seal with light thumbprint. Nose leather is seal or seal edged with pink. Paw pads are seal. Vivid blue eyes. Page 109.

62 Seal-Tortie Point Colorpoint Shorthair

Pale fawn to cream body shades to lighter undersides. Points are seal-brown mottled with red and/or cream. Facial blaze desirable. Nose leather and paw pads are seal, preferably with flesh or coral-pink mottling. Vivid blue eyes. Page 109.

64 Red Point Colorpoint Shorthair

Clear white body with shading in same tone as point color. Points are bright apricot to deep red, deeper shades preferred. Nose leather and paw pads are flesh or coral-pink. Vivid blue eyes. Page 109.

65 Red Ticked Tabby Oriental Shorthair

Red ground with dark red tabby markings and dark red tipping. Face, legs, and tail have tabby stripes. At least 1 necklace required. Nose leather and paw pads are brick-red. Green eyes. Page 120.

67 Chestnut Smoke Oriental Shorthair

White undercoat, deeply tipped with chestnut-brown so that cat at rest appears solid chestnut. White undercoat shows when cat moves. Nose leather and paw pads are lavender-pink. Green eyes. Page 120.

66 Chestnut Spotted Tabby Oriental Shorthair

Warm fawn ground with rich chestnut tabby markings. Nose leather is chestnut or pink edged with chestnut. Paw pads are cinnamon. Green eyes.
Page 120.

68 Ebony Oriental Shorthair

Jet-black coat from roots to tips. Nose leather is black. Paw pads are black or brown. Green eyes.
Page 120.

69 Havana Brown

Rich, even shade of warm sienna-brown overall, including nose leather, which has a rosy flush, and paw pads, also with a rosy tone. Whiskers must be brown. Green eyes.
Page 114.

71 Blue Ocicat

Dark blue spots show clearly on pale blue ground. Nose leather and paw pads are also blue. Yellow eyes.
Page 119.

70 Silver Egyptian Mau

Pale silver ground with dark charcoal markings. Black outlines nose, lips, and eyes. Nose leather is brick-red. Paw pads, between toes, and lower hind legs are black. Gooseberry-green eyes. Page 112.

72 Singapura

Ivory, yellow-tinged ground with brown ticking. Chin, chest, and stomach are color of unbleached muslin. Brown outlines eyes, nose, and lips. Nose leather is salmon. Paw pads are rosy brown. Hazel, green, or yellow eyes. Page 124.

73 Calico Cornish Rex

White with patches of black and red. White predominates on undersides and legs. Nose leather and paw pads are generally pink, but may be red, black, or combination of colors. Gold eyes. Page 110.

75 Blue Mackerel Tabby Cornish Rex

Pale bluish-ivory ground including lips and chin, with strongly contrasting dark blue tabby markings. Overall warm fawn patina. Nose leather is old rose. Paw pads are rose. Gold eyes. Page 110.

74 Black and White Cornish Rex

White and black with distinct areas of each color. Nose leather and paw pads are usually pink. Gold eyes. Page 110.

76 Red Classic Tabby Cornish Rex

Rich, dark red markings on red ground. Red lips and chin. Nose leather and paw pads are brick-red. Gold eyes. Page 110.

77 Tortoiseshell Devon Rex

Black with patches of red and cream. Red or cream facial blaze desirable. Nose leather and paw pads are usually black or mottled pink and black. Gold eyes. Page 111.

79 Brown Patched Mackerel Tabby and White American Wirehair

White chest, muzzle, undersides, legs, and feet. Tabby patches consisting of copper-brown ground with black mackerel tabby stripes and patches of red and cream. Nose leather is brick-red. Paw pads are black or brown. Gold eyes. Page 104.

78 Cream Smoke Devon Rex

White undercoat, deeply tipped with cream, so that cat at rest appears cream-colored. Mask, ears, legs, feet, and tail are cream. Nose leather and paw pads are rose. Gold eyes.
Page 111.

80 Brown Patched Mackerel Tabby American Wirehair

Dense black mackerel tabby markings on a copper-brown ground. Lips and chin match color of rings around eyes. Back of legs, from paw to heel, is black. Nose leather is brick-red. Paw pads are black or brown. Gold eyes.
Page 104.

81 Silver Classic Tabby American Shorthair

Pale, clear silver ground, including lips and chin, with dense black classic tabby markings. Nose leather is brick-red. Paw pads are black. Green or hazel eyes. Page 103.

83 Cameo Classic Tabby American Shorthair

Off-white ground with red-tipped classic tabby markings. Nose leather and paw pads are rose. Gold eyes. Page 103.

82 Red Classic Tabby American Shorthair

Deep, rich red classic tabby markings on red ground. Nose leather and paw pads are brick-red. Copper eyes.
Page 103.

84 Cream Mackerel Tabby American Shorthair

Very pale cream ground extends to lips and chin. Contrasting markings are darker buff or cream. Nose leather and paw pads are pink. Gold eyes.
Page 103.

85 Black Smoke American Shorthair

White undercoat, deeply tipped with black, so that cat at rest appears black. Undercoat shows when cat moves. Nose leather and paw pads are black. Gold eyes.
Page 103.

87 Blue British Shorthair

Light to medium blue coat. Lighter shades preferred, but evenness of color is more important than hue. Nose leather and paw pads are blue. Gold or copper eyes.
Page 106.

86 Black British Shorthair

Jet-black coat from roots to tips. Nose leather is also black. Paw pads are black or brown. Gold or copper eyes. Page 106.

88 Blue-Cream British Shorthair

Blue and cream are softly mingled, not patched. Nose leather and paw pads are blue and/or pink. Gold eyes. Page 106.

89 Blue and White British Shorthair

Blue and white combined in reasonably equal proportions. White facial blaze desirable. Nose leather and paw pads are usually pink. Gold eyes.
Page 106.

91 Chocolate Point Snowshoe

White muzzle, chin, chest, and feet in marked contrast to chocolate-brown points and dark saddle. Body is lighter color with subtle shading. Nose leather is pink or mottled pink and chocolate. Paw pads are pink. Blue eyes.
Page 125.

90 White British Shorthair

Pure white coat. Nose leather and paw pads are pink. Eyes may be blue, gold, or copper. The odd-eyed white cat has a blue and a gold eye, each of equal color depth.
Page 106.

92 Korat

Luminous silver-blue, with pale silver tipping. Nose leather and lips are dark blue or lavender. Paw pads are dark blue to lavender, with pink tinge. Green eyes preferred; amber cast acceptable.
Page 116.

93 Blue Exotic Shorthair

Light, even blue from nose to tip of tail preferred; darker shades acceptable. Nose leather and paw pads are blue. Copper eyes.
Page 113.

95 Black Smoke Exotic Shorthair

White undercoat, deeply tipped with black, so that cat at rest appears black. Undercoat shows when cat moves. Points are black. Nose leather and paw pads are black. Copper eyes.
Page 113.

94 Blue-Cream Exotic Shorthair

Blue with patches of cream on body and extremities. Nose leather and paw pads are blue and/or pink. Copper eyes. Page 113.

96 Smoke Tortoiseshell Exotic Shorthair

White undercoat tipped with black, red, and cream patches, creating tortoiseshell pattern. White ruff and ear tufts. Facial blaze of red or cream tipping desirable. Nose leather and paw pads vary. Copper eyes. Page 113.

97 White Exotic Shorthair

Pure, glistening white all over, with pink nose leather and paw pads. Blue or copper eyes or one of each color, with equal depth of color.
Page 113.

99 Black and White Scottish Fold

Black and white coat. Inverted "V" facial blaze desirable. Nose leather and paw pads are variable. Gold eyes.
Page 122.

98 Red Classic Tabby Exotic Shorthair

Red ground including lips and chin, with classic tabby markings in darker red. Nose leather and paw pads are brick-red. Copper eyes.
Page 113.

100 Brown Mackerel Tabby and White Scottish Fold

Patches of brown mackerel tabby and solid white. Copper-brown tabby ground has narrow, dense black mackerel markings. Nose leather and paw pads harmonize with surrounding color. Gold eyes.
Page 122.

101 Red Mackerel Tabby and White Manx

Narrow, dark red pencilings on red ground form mackerel tabby patches, which alternate with white patches. Nose leather and paw pads harmonize with surrounding color. Copper eyes. Page 118.

103 Brown Mackerel Tabby Manx

Narrow black mackerel tabby pencilings on copper-brown ground. Lips and chin match color of rings around eyes. Back of legs, from paw to heel, is black. Nose leather is brick-red. Paw pads are brown or black. Copper eyes. Page 118.

102 Red Classic Tabby Manx

Light red ground, including lips and chin, with dark, rich red classic tabby markings. Nose leather and paw pads are brick-red. Copper eyes.
Page 118.

104 Black and White Manx

Black and white coat in approximately equal amounts. Nose leather and paw pads are pink and/or black. Copper eyes.
Page 118.

105 Black Manx

Black coat from roots to tips. Nose leather is black. Paw pads are black or brown. Copper eyes.
Page 118.

107 Mi-Ke Japanese Bobtail

Black, red, and white, each color in striking contrast. Any color may predominate. Nose leather and paw pads harmonize with coat color. Eyes may be any color, including blue or odd-eyed.
Page 115.

106 Sphynx

Completely hairless black and white cat. Nose leather, paw pads, and eyes may be any color.
Page 126.

108 Red and White Japanese Bobtail

White with deep, brilliant red patches. Nose leather and paw pads harmonize with coat color. Eyes may be any color, including blue or odd-eyed.
Page 115.

Longhair Cats

Breeds
Balinese and Javanese
Birman
Cymric
Himalayan and Kashmir
Maine Coon
Norwegian Forest Cat
Persian
Ragdoll
Somali
Tiffany
Turkish Angora

Longhair Cats

Breed Status

There are thirteen breeds of cats generally classified as longhairs, and not all of these have achieved championship recognition by the Cat Fanciers' Association (CFA), the largest of the cat-registering associations. The six longhair breeds with full breed status are the Balinese, Birman, Maine Coon, Persian, Somali, and Turkish Angora. The Himalayan and Kashmir are included in the CFA's Persian division, but they have separate breed status in some other organizations. Five other breeds—the Cymric, Javanese, Norwegian Forest Cat, Ragdoll, and Tiffany—are in various stages of development here and abroad.

The Oldest Longhair Cats: Persians and Angoras

In terms of continuous development, the Persian is probably the oldest longhair breed. From the inception of cat shows in England more than 125 years ago, the Persians have been highly prized as companions. Early cats of this breed bore little resemblance to present-day Persians, although the standard of perfection has remained essentially the same. Perhaps the stability of the standard accounts for the large number of Persians that possess the round, full eyes; short, snub, broad nose; massive round head; and short, heavily boned, wide-set legs. The Persian standard also calls for small ears, a feature difficult to achieve in cats. The face has a sweet expression characterized by refined, undistorted, symmetrical features. Reported to be similar in type to the Persians of that era, the Angoras (later renamed Turkish Angoras) were also present in the earliest cat shows both here and in England. It was noted that only an expert could tell the difference, the fur of the Persian having been described as much more woolly than that of the Angora. A test to determine whether the cat was Persian or Angora

consisted of drawing the tail between the thumb and forefinger. Standards stated that the tail of the Angora would feel thin, silky, and narrow but would immediately "fluff" up. The Persian tail, on the other hand, "would not readily compress into a small space." The original Persian had a larger head and was "apparently stronger made" than the Angora.

These two similar breeds of cats became popular at the turn of the century. They have since developed into very distinct varieties. For a while the Angora was interbred with Persians and at one time almost lost recognition as a separate breed. Only the influence of the zoo in Ankara, Turkey, which housed and bred white Angoras, assured the Angora's preservation. Several pairs were imported from this source and used to develop the breed into a graceful, rather stylized version of the original. A small to medium-size wedge-shaped head with erect, pointed, and tufted ears presents a classic image of the Angora. It now bears no similarity to the Persian.

Himalayan and Kashmir

The first planned major longhair hybridization led to a Persian-type cat with Siamese coloring—the Himalayan. During the development of this new type with a point-restricted pattern, solid chocolate and lilac cats were produced that are now called Kashmirs in some associations. Today, Himalayans are very popular, second only to Persians in the number of longhair cats recorded.

Balinese and Javanese

Although the breed standard for the Balinese also calls for a long coat, the effect of this silky coat cascading over a long, hard, muscular body creates an entirely different effect from the long coats of the Persian and the Himalayan. The Balinese was developed from litters of registered Siamese. With the exception of coat length, the breed has the same long, svelte body. Balinese with new, non-Siamese colors—such as red point, tortie point, and lynx point—have been given the name Javanese.

Somali
The Somali bears the same relationship to the Abyssinian as the Balinese does to the Siamese. The first Somali occurred in litters of registered Abyssinians. Both the Somali and the Abyssinian standards call for a medium-length coat. However, the preferred ruff and breeches give the Somali a longhair appearance. The distinctive, vibrant coloring of the ticked coat has attracted many to this breed.

Birman
A colorful legend dramatizes the origin of the Birman (Sacred Cat of Burma). A pair was believed to have been stolen from a Burmese temple and slipped into France on a yacht. The breed achieved recognition in France in 1925, but its championship status is relatively new here. This large, stocky cat is closely identified with the white "paint" on its feet. The matching "gloves" should extend to the third joint on each of the front paws; on the back feet, they should extend up the hock, ending in a point. This trait, coupled with the Siamese coloring and deep blue, almond-shaped eyes, has made the Birman a favorite.

Maine Coon
The Maine Coon is believed to have come to this country by way of the many early ships sailing from Europe. Having a cat on board helped protect the cargo from rodents; in fact, a ship cat was a prerequisite for obtaining insurance. The Maine Coon, noted for a shaggy coat and hardy adaptability, remained somewhat isolated in its New England popularity until the last decade or so. It has now established itself as the native American longhair cat.

Norwegian Forest Cat
The Norwegian Forest Cat looks remarkably similar to the Maine Coon, and perhaps they share a European ancestry. However, this is not certain. The Norwegian Forest Cat is a recent arrival to the United States, and exists in very small numbers here. In Norway it enjoys protection as a national cultural symbol. Known primarily for its warm, water-resistant coat, it has much the same hardy structure, strong hunting instincts, and high degree of intelligence as the Maine Coon.

Cymric
The Cymric, or longhair Manx, is born from registered Manx parents but set apart by its medium-length coat complete with breeches and ruff. Presently considered "Any Other Variety" of Manx for CFA competition purposes, it is gaining acceptance among cat fanciers. This powerfully built, tailless cat originated on the Isle of Man off the coast of England. The government there maintains a cattery, and many fanciers prefer to purchase stock developed at the source. Tourism on the island is highly developed around the many souvenir articles depicting tailless cats.

Ragdoll
The Ragdoll is a combination of the Birman, the Persian, and the shorthair Burmese breed and is currently not eligible for registration with the Cat Fanciers' Association. Registration is necessary for entry into the nonchampionship miscellaneous (developing) category, so the Ragdoll's future as a breed is not assured. Due to its mixed heritage, it may or may not have the "mitted" white feet that are the characteristic most commonly associated with the Ragdoll.

Tiffany
Like the Ragdoll, the Tiffany is a new breed, the status of which is still somewhat questionable. This longhair

sable cat was developed in England by mating Himalayans and Burmese. Few exist in the United States.

A Wide Range of Personalities

Variety abounds within the longhair breeds, and a compatible personality can easily be found. The Balinese, Javanese, Maine Coon, Norwegian Forest Cat, Turkish Angora, and Somali are all inventive and intensely curious. Quiet, assured dignity is more likely to be found among the Birman, Himalayan, Kashmir, Persian, and Ragdoll. The Cymric may be all of the above, depending on its audience and its mood.

Care for a Longhair Cat

The primary rule in caring for a longhair cat is to keep the coat clean and to comb it regularly to remove excess hair. Normally, a cat will shed during the spring. However, a spiky, unkempt coat may be a sign of illness and should be investigated by your veterinarian if it persists. Because most longhair cats have longer tufts of hair on their paws, it is necessary to watch the nails closely to prevent claws from growing into the paw pad, especially in older cats. Trim the tips of the claws with a small nail clipper once a week. Also, the inside of the ear should be kept clean and free of wax buildup and other matter, such as mites. These microscopic parasites leave a crumbly, dark residue similar to coffee grounds. Observe your cat for any excess scratching; a clean, healthy cat does not dig at its ears with its hind foot.

Cats do not have an odor associated with their bodies, as dogs do. Any noticeable odor from the mouth or coat should be investigated immediately. Mature male cats do develop a strong urine odor, and they may also spray to mark their territory. Longhairs are less likely to spray than the shorthair breeds, but males kept as pets should be neutered just prior to maturity. It is extremely rare for a longhair female to spray, but

for the well-being of the cat, it should be altered unless it was purchased to breed.

Exercise and Companionship

Regardless of the length of its coat, a cat needs space to play, climb, and stretch. Some breeds are more sedate and less vocal than others, but all need human companionship. Most longhair cats are ideal apartment dwellers and can adapt to the confines of a house or an apartment quickly. If you want them to be content inside, it is important not to introduce them to the outside.

Most longhair cats have very stable personalities and meld well into a family atmosphere. They are rarely destructive in their habits and lack the excitability of some of the shorthair breeds.

Balinese and Javanese

Characteristics
Draped, silky, fine, long coat
Deep blue eyes
Long, elegant lines
Long, triangular head

Personality
Warm, eager, and enthusiastic. Highly inquisitive. Never content to be observers. Want to participate in every activity. Insistent and vocal.

Ideal Appearance
Medium-size. Svelte, longhair cats with Siamese coat pattern. Fine, long, silky coat falls like cloak over sleek, muscular body. Fine bones and firm muscles. Long, slender legs with hind legs higher than front legs. Long, wedge-shaped head with large, pointed ears and almond-shaped eyes set at slant toward long nose. Slender long neck balances long, thin, plumed tail.

Colors
Balinese colors are seal point, chocolate point, blue point, and lilac point. Javanese colors include red, tortie, and lynx-point patterns. Color on diamond-shaped mask, ears, legs, feet, and tail strongly contrasts with pale, even body color. Eyes are deep vivid blue. Nose and paw pads match point color.

Potential Health Problems
Certain lines may have weak hind legs. Nasal obstruction or poor occlusion can cause breathing through mouth. Generally a healthy breed.

Care and Grooming
Long, silky coat needs occasional grooming with metal comb. Curiosity often leads cats into adventures requiring bath afterward. Need companionship and lots of opportunity for action. Provide heavy-duty scratching post, space to climb and play, and a variety of toys.

Kittens
Average litter from 4 to 6 kittens, but larger litters of 6 to 8 are not uncommon. Born cream-white; point color develops as kittens mature.

Comment
When the first longhair kitten appeared in a litter of pedigreed Siamese, it was considered a mutation. Over the years, as more longhair Siamese were born, they began to attract a following among American breeders. Inspired by the graceful movement of these long, svelte cats, advocates coined the name Balinese after the Balinese dancers. Some people theorized that the long hair was not a mutation at all but a recessive genetic characteristic that had reemerged from some distant longhair ancestor of the Siamese parents. Whatever the cause, breeders soon discovered that by mating 2 longhair Siamese, they could reliably produce Balinese kittens identical to the parents.

The Cat Fanciers' Association accepted Balinese for championship status in 1970 in the 4 Siamese colors. Other associations (but not the Cat Fanciers' Association) also recognize the red, tortie, and lynx-point patterns. The Cat Fanciers' Association calls these red or pattern-pointed cats Javanese and accepts them for registration but not for championship.

With the exception of its long, silky coat, the Balinese has the same characteristics as the Siamese, from its long, wedge-shaped head and sleek body to its deep blue, almond-shaped eyes.

Recommendation
The Balinese and Javanese are lively and persistent, with a wide variety of voices, from soft to noisy depending on their mood. Balanced and agile, they need space to run and exercise their long, muscular bodies. You can have no secrets from these cats; they will share all you do.

Plates 33, 34, 35, 36

Birman

Characteristics
White-gloved feet
Long, silky coat
Deep blue eyes
Inscrutable,
penetrating gaze

Personality
Sweet-natured and intelligent. Basically quiet and able to play by itself. When away from owners, may seem nostalgic. Appears conscious of its sacred origin. Has a quiet, clucking voice. Charming.

Ideal Appearance
Large to medium-size. Sturdy, stocky cat with long body. Long, silky coat with characteristic white-gloved feet; does not mat and is slightly curly on stomach. Strong, broad, rounded head with Roman nose and low-set nostrils. Full ruff around neck. Nearly round eyes and round-tipped, medium-size ears set as much on side as on top of broad head.

Colors
Seal point, chocolate point, blue point, and lilac point—all with white gloves. Front paws white to third joint. Back feet completely white up to hocks. Points contrast sharply with even body colors. Deep blue eyes. Pink nose leather and paw pads.

Potential Health Problems
Certain lines have genetic defects, such as weak hind legs or nasal obstruction and poor occlusion, which can cause breathing through the mouth.

Care and Grooming
Long, silky coat does not mat and therefore requires relatively little care. Occasional combing recommended. Bathe as necessary to keep coat free of grease. Watch for grease buildup under tail of males.

Kittens
Average litter 4 kittens. Color when born completely pale-cream; point color darkens with age. A trained eye can detect future level of white gloves when kittens are still wet.

Comment
Known as the Sacred Cat of Burma, this breed's origin is shrouded in mystery and intrigue. The original pair allegedly was stolen from the underground temple of Loa-Tsun in Burma. Since the cats were considered sacred by the Kittaha monks, their theft was a sacrilege. According to legend, those who cared for them were blessed and those who harmed them punished. Another story relates how a golden-eyed cat touched a holy man at the moment of his death, and the cat's feet became pure white where they rubbed his robe. As the cat turned its head from the dead holy man, its eyes turned the same deep blue as the sapphire eyes of the temple goddess. Thereafter, when a sacred cat died at the temple, it was believed that the soul of a holy man took its place in the paradise of Song-Hio, the golden god.
The Birman was first described by a major in the British army in 1898 but was not established as a breed until 1925, and then only in France. The breed was developed in the United States in the 1960s.

Recommendation
This extremely social cat should never be kept entirely in solitude. It needs the company of other pets and people and blends easily into a family environment.

Plates 23, 24

Cymric

Characteristics
Tailless
Stout
Hind legs higher than
front legs
Short back
Moderately long coat

Personality
Alert, intelligent, and sweet-natured.
Very quiet, with only an occasional
birdlike trill to express enthusiasm.

Ideal Appearance
Large. Tailless. Hair moderately long.
Round head and broad muzzle with
prominent cheeks. Short, balanced,
substantial front legs contrast with
higher, heavily muscled hindquarters.
Stout, heavy chest. Short back shows
smooth, continuous arch from shoulders
to rump. On mature cat, breeches should
be full and thick to hocks, giving
appearance of gaucho pants with boots.
Stomach, breeches, and neck ruff longer
than fur on rest of body. Fine, silky coat
falls smoothly; thick, plushy undercoat.

Colors
All colors are acceptable with the
exception of those showing
hybridization, such as chocolate,
lavender, ticked tabby, point-restricted
colors, or these colors in combination
with white. In this breed, color and
pattern are not very important for show
points. Nose leather, paw pads, and eyes
harmonize with coat color.

Potential Health Problems
Taillessness can be associated with
defects not always apparent in kittens
under 12 weeks of age. Be sure cat can
stand and walk properly. Watch for
weakness in hindquarters resulting in
lack of a proper gait. Should be able to
use hind legs independently without any
hint of limp. Certain lines prone to
incontinence.

Care and Grooming
Biweekly combing with wire-tooth metal
comb or brush maintains silky coat.
Comb armpits and stomach to prevent
matting. Comb and clip nail tips before
bathing. Herbal shampoos work well.
Due to double coat, it takes time to get
cat wet to the skin and shampooed.
Rinse very well and blot dry with a
towel. Comb through coat while still
wet. Use a quiet hair dryer.

Kittens
Litters average 4 large, hardy kittens.
Cymrics born with 1 of 4 tail lengths:
full tail (often docked at birth), natural
stump (short portion of tail), rumpy riser
(small sliver of bone fragment at base of
spine; can be lifted but not wagged), or
dimpled rumpy (complete absence of
tail, leaving an indentation where spine
ends). Dimpled rumpy and rumpy riser
most desirable.

Comment
The Cymric is a longhair Manx, born
only of purebred Manx parents, and it is
not considered a hybrid. During the
original breeding of Manx cats, on the
Isle of Man off the west coast of
England, some longhair cats occasionally
resulted due to recessive genes. Both
shorthair Manx parents must have the
longhair gene to produce Cymric
offspring. Cymrics bred to each other
produce only longhair kittens. Although
the Cymric is not recognized as a
separate breed by the Cat Fanciers'
Association, it is eligible for competition
as "Any Other Variety" of Manx. It is
recognized for championship competition
by several other associations, however,
including the American Cat Association
(ACA), the Canadian Cat Association
(CCA), and The International Cat
Association (TICA).

Recommendation
The Cymric is even-tempered and quiet,
extremely intelligent and observant.
Don't rush friendship. Given an
introductory period, the Cymric will
form a lifelong bond with its owner. Its
gentle, loving ways make it a good, low-
maintenance pet. It is excellent with
children, as well as with dogs and even
horses, and loves to entertain with its
clownlike antics.

Plates 1, 31, 32

Himalayan and Kashmir

Characteristics
Persian-type build
Himalayan has point
pattern
Kashmir is
chocolate or lilac

Personality
Intelligent and outgoing. Devoted, gentle, and affectionate. Can be quite demanding. Voice usually louder than that of a Persian but much quieter than their Siamese ancestors'.

Ideal Appearance
Medium-size to large. Essentially Persian type. Short, cobby body. Large head on short neck has snublike nose with good break. Small ears set low on head. Large, round eyes are expressive. Short, full tail in proportion to body length. Long, fine coat should appear full of life; ruff around neck.

Colors
Himalayan originally available in only 2 colors, seal point and blue point; range now includes chocolate point, lilac point, flame (red) point, cream point, tortie point, blue-cream point, and, more recently, seal-lynx point and blue-lynx point. Show standard for all point colors requires deep vivid blue eyes. Solid colors of chocolate or lilac are known as Kashmirs in some associations. These 2 colors do not have points and are a single, even shade. Nose leather and paw pads harmonize with coat color. Eyes are copper. Both Himalayans and Kashmirs are considered part of the Persian division of the Cat Fanciers' Association.

Potential Health Problems
Usually healthy. Very short nose may be associated with tearing because of malformed tear ducts. Breathing problems also possible in some lines.

Care and Grooming
Daily grooming essential to prevent or remove tangles from long coat. Use 2 steel combs, 1 with wide-set teeth and 1 with narrow teeth, plus a grooming brush. Regular bathing is recommended. Light powdering of body will help keep it free from tangles. Face and eyes should be wiped with washcloth to remove stains.

Kittens
Average litter 4 kittens, although only 1 is not unusual. Kashmirs are born solid color and darken with age. Himalayan kittens are born pure white with nose and paw pads bright pink. Point coloring starts to develop after a few days; color of points can be seen clearly at 4 weeks.

Comment
Developed in Britain and North America in the 1930s, the Himalayan is a Persian-type cat with a long, flowing coat and a Siamese pattern. It is not a longhair Siamese like the Balinese breed. The idea of crossing 2 such different breeds as the Persian and Siamese was highly unusual, since the bone structures of these cats are completely opposite: the Persian is short, cobby, and heavy-boned, whereas the Siamese is long, svelte, and has fine bones. After many years of selective breeding, the Himalayan gained championship recognition in 1955 in Britain and in 1957 in the United States. During the development of chocolate-point and lilac-point Himalayans, solid chocolate and solid lilac cats often resulted. Both of these solid-color Himalayans are called Kashmirs in some associations, although the Cat Fanciers' Association considers them to be a division of the Persian. Good examples of these breathtaking colors are rare.

Recommendation
Easygoing cats, the Himalayan and Kashmir fit in well with family life and purr loudly in appreciation of attention. They prefer a regular routine. Although these breeds can adapt to apartment living if provided with toys to encourage exercise, they need lots of space in which to run and play. Both get along well with other pets.

Plates 5, 6, 7, 8, 9, 20

Maine Coon

Characteristics
Shaggy coat
Large, muscular
Broad-chested
High cheekbones
Square muzzle
Large, well-tufted,
high-set ears

Personality
Amiable, hardy, and outgoing, with casual, easygoing attitude. Self-assured demeanor. In control of most situations. Adapts to other animals. Thrives in a family environment. Great hunter. Enjoys retrieval games. Tiny voice; squeaks, chirps, and trills.

Ideal Appearance
Large, often 12 to 18 pounds. Medium-wide head. Medium-long nose. Large, tufted, tall ears. High cheekbones accent large, wide-set, slightly oblique eyes. Muscular and broad-chested, with substantial, wide-set legs and large, round, well-tufted paws. Flowing fur on long, tapering tail is often, according to climate conditions, the single factor signifying that the Maine Coon is a longhair breed. Characteristic heavy, shaggy coat falls smoothly. Coat is short on shoulders, longer on stomach and breeches. Frontal ruff is desirable.

Colors
Best known for the brown tabby variety, Maine Coons come in a broad range of colors and patterns: solid white, black, blue, red, or cream; classic or mackerel tabby in red, brown, blue, or cream; tortoiseshell and blue-cream; calico, dilute calico, bicolor, or particolor (with approximately one-third white); chinchilla, shaded silver, shell cameo, shaded cameo, black smoke, blue smoke, and cameo smoke. Any solid colors, tabby patterns, or tortoiseshell and blue-cream may be combined with white. Unlike all other breeds, eye color varies from green to gold to copper and is not related to coat color.

Potential Health Problems
Generally quite hardy. Certain lines have recently produced kittens with flattened chest structure; although fine as pets these should not be used for breeding. Kinked tails are a common genetic defect.

Care and Grooming
Comb weekly and bathe as required. Check teeth regularly for tartar. Gums should be healthy pink without red lines or spots.

Kittens
Average litter of 4 kittens, but 6 to 8 not uncommon. Slow to mature; full size not usually reached until 4 to 5 years old. Every kitten in the litter may be different in coat color and pattern.

Comment
The Maine Coon, considered to be the native American longhair cat, first appeared on the rocky coast of New England. Its ancestors may have been ratters on early ships to the New World. Its raccoonlike (brown tabby) color pattern and large size may have contributed to its name. Shown in the earliest United States cat shows, the breed fell into obscurity when cat fanciers began to import Persians and Siamese. The breed continued to flourish in its original northeastern habitat and was shown and admired at local shows in the 1950s. After it was granted championship status by the Cat Fanciers' Association in 1976, the Maine Coon's popularity greatly increased.

Recommendation
Amiable and lovable, the Maine Coon requires little maintenance. It is family oriented and happiest with another pet or person for companionship and stimulation. Originally a working cat, this solid, rugged breed can endure a harsh climate, but is also able to adapt to milder climates.

Plates 3, 25, 26, 27, 28

Norwegian Forest Cat

Characteristics
Shaggy, water-
resistant double coat
Long, flowing tail
Toe tufts
Tiptoe gait

Personality
Exceedingly alert. Responsive and loving
to its owner. Has speed, courage, and
intelligence necessary for survival in
extreme conditions of Norwegian
woodlands. Creative, innovative hunting
instincts.

Ideal Appearance
Medium-size to large. Almost
equilaterally triangular head. Almond-
shaped, expressive eyes set on slight
angle. Body moderately long. Powerful
appearance due to full chest and
considerable girth. Hind legs higher
than front, with heavily muscled thighs.
Long, flowing tail carried high. Long,
rich fur with light, woolly undercoat and
oily outer (guard) hairs. Ruff has 3
sections: full frontal bib, side mutton
chops, and short back-of-the-neck
fullness. In summer, only ear and toe
tufts and tail distinguish Norwegian
Forest Cat as a longhair.

Colors
All color combinations are accepted,
with or without white, except for the
Himalayan pattern. White buttons and
small lockets are allowed in tabbies only,
although those without this trait are
preferred. Tabbies with white or off-
white chin, breast, and stomach are
allowed, although not desirable. Nose
leather, paw pads, and eyes harmonize
with coat color.

Potential Health Problems
Rare instances of flattened chest.
Generally a hardy breed, although its
health history is not well known in this
country.

Care and Grooming
Coat is warm and water-resistant; does
not tangle, lump, or mat and requires
relatively little grooming. Occasional
combing removes loose hairs and thereby
helps prevent hair balls. Shampooing,
however, can remove oil that makes coat
water-resistant. Strong, thick claws are
difficult to trim but should be cared for
at least every 2 weeks.

Kittens
Litters usually of 4 to 6 kittens. Very
slow to mature; full muscular
development of neck and body does not
occur until cat is 4 to 5 years old.

Comment
Although centuries old in Norway, the
Norwegian Forest Cat is relatively new
in the United States and not recognized
for show status by the Cat Fanciers'
Association. It is eligible for
championship in some other associations.
Called a *Skogkatt* in Norway, the breed is
of unknown origin. It does predate the
introduction of the Persian into Norway
and is not basically a Persian hybrid. The
cat is mentioned in Norse mythology and
is referred to as a "fairy cat" in fairy tales
recorded in the mid-19th century. The
numerous cats that lived in the
Norwegian woodlands away from the
coastline once faced extinction and exist
today only through crossbreeding with
other cats. In the early 1970s, the
Norwegians attempted to preserve this
breed as a living monument to the
national culture.

Recommendation
The high intelligence the Norwegian
Forest Cat found necessary for survival
translates into fascinating pet behavior.
Extremely adaptable, this cat is inventive
about opening doors and latches. Get a
Norwegian Forest Cat only if you can
provide the companionship it needs,
because it refuses solitude.

Plate 22

Persian

Characteristics
Short, cobby body
Long, flowing coat
with ruff
Massive head with
small ears
Large, expressive eyes
Full tail

Personality
Well mannered and quiet. Melodious voice. Excellent companion, loves attention. When picked up, it will often wrap its paws around owner's neck, nudging and butting with its head amid thunderous purrs of appreciation. Some develop endearing quality of sitting up on haunches to beg like a little bear. Less active than shorthair breeds due to heavier, stocky body and short, sturdy legs. Playful but not demanding.

Ideal Appearance
Large to medium-size. Massive, round head set on short, thick neck. Small, round-tipped ears set far apart and low on head. Short, broad, snub nose with a deep break. Large, round eyes give sweet expression to face, which has full cheeks and powerful jaw. Classic cobby build: like a box. Very short in body, low on legs with a good width to chest. Legs short, thick, and strong. Tail referred to as "brush": very full, short. Long, fine-textured coat is full of life, standing out from body. Immense ruff forms deep frill between front legs. Long ear tufts and toe tufts.

Colors
Persian colors are split into 6 CFA divisions for show purposes: solid colors, including solid chocolate and lilac; shaded (tipped) colors; smokes, tabby patterns; particolors; and point-restricted colors. Most other associations recognize the point-restricted colors as Himalayan and the chocolate and the lilac as Kashmir (see Himalayan and Kashmir account). Solid-color Persians are white, black, blue, red, or cream, plus chocolate or lilac. All have copper eyes except whites, which may have blue, copper, or odd eyes. Shaded (tipped) colors include chinchilla, shaded silver, golden chinchilla, and shaded golden (all 4 with green or blue-green eyes); shell cameo, shaded cameo, shell tortoiseshell, or shaded tortoiseshell (with brilliant copper eyes). Smokes include black smoke, blue smoke, cameo smoke, tortoiseshell smoke, and blue-cream smoke. (All of these have copper eyes.) The tabby colors include silver, red, brown, blue, cream, or cameo in either the classic or mackerel tabby patterns. (All should have brilliant copper eyes except the silver tabby, which must have green or hazel eyes.) Patched tabbies come in silver, brown, or blue. Particolors include tortoiseshell, calico, dilute calico, blue-cream, or bicolors— such as black and white, blue and white, red and white, cream and white—plus the tabby and white class. (All of these have copper eyes.)

Potential Health Problems
Generally healthy. Some white cats, including Persians, are born deaf. This usually occurs in cats with blue or odd eyes; odd-eyed cats may be deaf only on blue-eyed side. Deaf cats should be kept indoors at all times for their protection. Certain lines with very flat faces may have breathing problems or difficulty with clogged tear ducts. Possible entropion cataracts are very rare.

Care and Grooming
Requires daily grooming with steel comb. A little knot in fur will soon become large tangle if left unattended and will cause pain as it pulls against tender skin. Powder lightly with French chalk or baby powder to keep hair separated. Regular bathing usually necessary to remove excess oil from coat. It is easier to care for young kittens and cats not being shown if hair under tail is clipped. Short nose puts pressure on tear ducts and can cause eyes to run. This can stain fur on face and on front paws when cat washes its face; particularly noticeable on white and light-colored cats. Gently wipe away stains daily with damp washcloth. Black, blue, and related colors tend to show rusty tinges if cat sits too long in sun.

Kittens

Average litter 3 or 4 kittens, although number varies greatly. Females often need assistance delivering and cleaning newborn kittens. Once kittens are cleaned, mother will accept and nurse them. Generally good mothers, Persians enjoy their young and keep them spotlessly clean. Often the contented kittens are reluctant to leave the nest.

Comment

The Persian is one of the oldest and most popular breeds. Although its exact origin is not known, longhair cats were mentioned in a publication by the French naturalist De Buffon in the late 18th century. According to Italian sources, longhair cats were introduced into Italy even earlier—in the late 1500s —probably from Asia.

Many early records refer to the cats as Angoras. Early British books on cats referred to them as French cats, and they were believed to have come from Ankara, Turkey. These cats had small heads, tall ears, and rangy bodies. Later, other longhairs came from Persia (Iran), but these differed considerably in body structure. They had sturdier bodies, shorter legs, broader, rounder heads, and longer fur of a different texture. The two breeds were interbred, but because the Persian type was preferred, the Angora type quickly disappeared from the Persian breed. The Angora is now popular as a separate breed and is known as the Turkish Angora.

At the first official cat show in Britain in 1871, Persian exhibits were mostly black, blue, or white cats; other colors were gradually added. However, the blue became the most popular in that era, no doubt in part because Queen Victoria and other members of royalty owned blue Persians. Cats of excellent quality were exported around the world, and present-day Persians are descended mostly from those early British cats.

Recommendation

An easygoing, quiet cat, the Persian adapts well to apartment living. It likes to be close to its owner. It can happily be the only pet, but it will also get along well with other animals. A future owner should be prepared to spend time each day grooming this breed's magnificent full coat.

Plates 4, 10–19

Ragdoll

Characteristics
Heavy, powerful
build
Medium to long,
thick, silky coat
Blue eyes
Docile disposition

Personality
Docile and imperturbable. People-oriented. Loves retrieval and other games. Quiet unless excited; can be noisy when unhappy.

Ideal Appearance
Exceptionally large and heavy. Large, oval, blue eyes. Medium-size ears set high on modified wedge-shaped head. Nose twice as long as it is wide, with gentle break. Firm and muscular. Cat in repose shows subdued power. Broad at the chest and hindquarters. High hindquarters make back appear to tilt forward slightly. Large, round, tufted paws balance heavy-boned, medium-length legs. Medium to long coat.

Colors
Seal point, chocolate point, blue point, and lilac point in 3 distinctly marked patterns. In the first pattern there may be no white. The second, or mitted, pattern has white mittens or gloves in addition to color points and a white stripe of varying widths that extends from the bib, between the legs, to under the tail. The third or bicolor pattern has colored points with white on legs, chest, and stomach. Eyes are blue in all colors and patterns.

Potential Health Problems
Like all cats, needs routine teeth cleaning and check-ups. As it is a new breed, health history is unknown.

Care and Grooming
Requires low maintenance due to nonmatting texture of coat, but combing needed to keep shedding to minimum and help prevent hair balls. Bathe as necessary to keep cat clean and well-groomed. Annual dental checkups advised. Although this cat is one of the largest domestic breeds, it makes no special space demands.

Kittens
Average 4 kittens per litter. Kittens are born creamy white with point color; pattern increases in intensity until maturity. Need to nurse and remain with mother longer than most breeds. Very slow to mature; size and muscular development not apparent for several years.

Comment
The Ragdoll is a hybrid breed resulting from the mating of a white Persian and a seal point Birman. That progeny was then mated to a sable Burmese, thereby establishing the original Ragdoll lines in the 1960s. Controversy exists as to how many different breed characteristics should be combined in the development of an acceptable breed. Ragdolls are not recognized by the Cat Fanciers' Association; however, they are acceptable in several other associations.

Recommendation
Before investing large amounts of money in a Ragdoll, investigate its background carefully. Those advocating the Ragdoll claim that it has a remarkable disposition and intelligence.

Plate 37

Somali

Characteristics
Medium-size
Lithe and muscular
Easy to groom,
medium-length coat
Even disposition
Easy to handle

Personality
Friendly and affectionate. Likes attention. Playful, intelligent, and very active, but gentle and soft-voiced. Demonstrative.

Ideal Appearance
Medium-size. Overall type is the same as the Abyssinian, but with medium-long silky coat and foxlike tail. Head shows a modified wedge shape without flat planes. Ears large, alert, and moderately pointed. Large, almond-shaped, expressive eyes. Firm and muscular body is lithe, graceful, and elegant. Full brush tail thick at base and tapering. Medium-length double coat. Hair ticked with 3 bands of color, giving an agouti appearance. Coat longer on ruff and breeches. Coat is very soft to the touch and extremely fine.

Colors
2 special breed colors: ruddy and red, both with gold or green eyes, the deeper the better. Ruddy is orange-brown, ticked with black. Ears and tail are tipped with black, while undersides of body and inside legs and chest are an even ruddy tone, without ticking. Nose leather is tile-red; paw pads black or brown. Red is warm and glowing, ticked with chocolate-brown; deeper shades of red preferred. Ears and tail are tipped with chocolate-brown. Nose leather and paw pads are rosy pink. Any white spots or white anywhere except upper throat, chin, and nostrils disqualify.

Potential Health Problems
Usually hardy. As with all cats, teeth and gums should be checked regularly for signs of inflammation.

Care and Grooming
Silky, medium-length coat does not tangle easily, but groom daily with good steel comb to keep it in good condition. Bathe regularly to keep coat free of greasy texture and help prevent stud tail. If grooming brush is used, it should be of natural bristle and used sparingly in order not to break hair and spoil ticking.

Kittens
Average litter 2 or 3 kittens, with more males than females. Most kittens are slow to develop full coat coloring and ticking. Kittens are strong and active.

Comment
When longhair kittens started appearing in Abyssinian litters in the 1960s, they were at first thought to be natural mutations. However, it was later discovered that many of the ancestors of these longhairs could be traced, through British and other overseas imports, to breeds that had longhairs many generations back in their pedigrees. Through inbreeding, the recessive gene brought back the longhair influence to create the Somali. This gene must be present in both parents to produce Somalis. Somalis may be bred back to Abyssinians to improve the type, but all resulting kittens will be shorthaired, with some carrying the Somali gene. The only way to guarantee an all-Somali litter is by breeding Somali to Somali. The breed achieved CFA championship status in 1978.

Recommendation
This breed requires freedom and lots of space for exercise. It does not thrive in a cage, where it will pace like a wild animal. The Somali prefers company, either human or another pet.

Plates 29, 30

Tiffany

Characteristics
Longhair version of
Burmese
Relatively long coat
Docile
Conversational

Personality
Gentle and soft-voiced. Chirps rather than meows. Enjoys conversation. Similar to Burmese but more docile. Quite playful.

Ideal Appearance
Medium-size like Burmese. Oriental body type. Cobby, but slightly higher on hind legs. Main difference is coat length. Coat is medium-long and silky, resembling that of Turkish Angora. Modified neck ruff. Foxlike facial expression, with round eyes.

Colors
Sable only, with gold eyes. Color resembles sable Burmese, except paw pads are pink like chocolate Himalayan.

Potential Health Problems
Few examples exist in this country, so medical history is unknown.

Care and Grooming
Medium-length coat needs little care beyond routine combing. Pay particular attention to tail and hindquarters, where hair tends to mat. Little shedding.

Kittens
Average 3 to litter. Born café au lait, color darkening as they mature. Shadow point color and/or tabby markings disappear as body color intensifies. Kittens are fuzzy. At first only indication of potential long hair is on tail. Coat length comes in at about 10 months.

Comment ⇥
At one time believed to be a spontaneous mutation, the Tiffany is now known to result from a recessive longhair gene. The original Tiffanies were produced in England by crossing Himalayans and Burmese during early attempts to develop solid chocolate Himalayans (now called Kashmirs). During the past 20 years, the number of longhair sable kittens that have popped up in Burmese litters has been much less frequent; thus fewer Tiffanies are available. The breed was introduced in the United States by a Florida breeder who is still the only person perpetuating a breeding program here. The Tiffany is not currently registered in any association, since it was dropped by the American Cat Association for lack of numbers.

Recommendation
A pleasant pet, the Tiffany is relaxed and devoted to its owner. It is less active than the Burmese and likes people. Some people appreciate the breed's doglike mannerisms—following its owner around like a puppy.

Plate 21

Turkish Angora

Characteristics
Radiant, almond-shaped eyes
Pointed, erect, tufted ears
Fine, silky sheen
Medium-long coat
Long and lithe

Personality
Polite and courteous. Readily understands owner's desires. Intelligent and responsive. Easily trained to retrieve and perform tricks. Fastidious; prefers spotless environment. Loves water and has been known to play in the tub, but prefers to choose where to bathe.

Ideal Appearance
Small to medium-size. A solid, firm cat giving impression of grace and flowing movement. Large, erect, tufted ears set high on small to medium-size, wedge-shaped head. Large, almond-shaped eyes show radiant, deep color. Long, lithe, graceful torso with light frame. Hind legs higher than front legs. Long, full tail often carried high or almost touching head. Fine, medium-long coat with silky, wavy tendency. Not as full as most longhairs. No woolly undercoat. Ruff should be long.

Colors
Once bred only for white coat with amber, blue, or odd eyes, the breed currently also includes solids in black, blue, cream, or red; classic or mackerel tabby patterns in silver, red, brown, blue, or cream; tortoiseshell, calico, dilute calico, blue-cream, and bicolors— black, blue, red, or cream with white.

Potential Health Problems
Usually strong and hardy. Blue-eyed white cats are often deaf, and odd-eyed cats may be deaf on blue-eyed side. Deafness possible in other colors.

Care and Grooming
Routine inspection of teeth and gums advised to prevent buildup of tartar. Bathe a few days before show or hair will have flyaway look. Relatively little grooming required.

Kittens
Litters average 4 kittens. Slow to mature; may not achieve full coat until 2 years of age. Precocious.

Comment
Originally called Ankara cats, the breed comes from the province of Ankara, in Turkey. Angora-type cats are mentioned in early 19th-century documents, and nearly a century later some were shown in the first American cat shows. The breed was faced with extinction at the turn of the century due to crossbreeding with Persian cats. Later the zoo in Ankara helped preserve the Angora by maintaining it in a controlled breeding environment. Only the whites with amber, blue, or odd eyes were kept by the zoo, although books written at the turn of the century indicate that cats in other colors also existed. The Angora breed of today can be traced to 2 unrelated pairs of cats brought into the United States from that zoo in the 1960s.

Recommendation
This sociable cat thrives especially well in a one-pet household. Males are generally less nervous than females. Charming and inventive, Turkish Angoras are good hunters and enjoy repetitive routines and games.

Plates 2, 38, 39, 40

Shorthair Cats

Breeds
Abyssinian
American Shorthair
American Wirehair
Bombay
British Shorthair
Burmese
Chartreux
Colorpoint Shorthair
Cornish Rex
Devon Rex
Egyptian Mau
Exotic Shorthair
Havana Brown
Japanese Bobtail
Korat
Malayan
Manx
Ocicat
Oriental Shorthair
Russian Blue
Scottish Fold
Siamese
Singapura
Snowshoe
Sphynx
Tonkinese

Shorthair Cats

Ancient Beginnings

Cats—domesticated and deified—are depicted in murals, amulets, and scrolls from the time when the pharaohs ruled the Nile Valley. These illustrations show that the cats of ancient Egypt were decidedly shorthaired, a fact borne out by mummified examples found in that civilization's tombs. Egyptian papyrus scrolls and temple paintings from as long ago as 1400 B.C. contain illustrations of cats—spotted tabbies—that are thought to represent the breed known today as the Egyptian Mau. The history of the Abyssinian is probably at least as ancient.

All domestic cats almost certainly descended from the North African wild cat, *Felis libyca*. They were probably first taken into human custody about 1600 B.C., when the silo was invented and cats were employed to eliminate rodents from grain stores. It is likely that domestic cats made their way from Egypt to other parts of the world by way of Phoenician traders. The ever-conquering, ever-traveling Romans, in their turn, probably introduced the domesticated shorthair cat nearly two thousand years ago to northern Europe and the British Isles, where at that time wild cats were apparently better known.

In the Orient the cat had long been an honored creature. Recorded in the *Cat-Book Poems,* manuscripts dated A.D. 1350 to 1767 found in Ayutthaya, the ancient capital of Siam (now Thailand), are cats native to that land at the time. Among them are described and depicted some all-brown cats, probably relatives of today's Burmese and Tonkinese, that were said to protect their owners from evil. The silver-blue Si-Sawat, or Korat, is described as a good-luck cat. Included, too, are cats of other colors that are probably our Oriental Shorthairs. But it was the point-restricted cats—the ancestors of what are known today as Siamese—that seem to have been especially revered, even by royalty, who apparently kept them as pets.

Despite historical or biological fact, the origins and diversity of cat breeds have long been the stuff of legends. Of the shorthairs, myth would have it that the Siamese cat is the descendant of an Egyptian goddess named Bast, and that the Manx cat is tailless because Noah slammed the door of the Ark too soon. Genes and evolution, of course, are the scientific reality behind these myths. But were it not for the desire to improve upon nature, cats as we know them today would not exist; certainly not the approximately twenty-six purebred shorthair breeds.

A Diverse Selection

The Cat Fanciers' Association, the largest cat-registering organization, recognizes twenty breeds for championship status and classifies one other, the Malayan, as a division of the accepted Burmese breed. Five shorthair breeds that are not recognized by the Cat Fanciers' Association—the Chartreux, Ocicat, Singapura, Snowshoe, and Sphynx—are also included here.

Shorthair breeds can be divided into four basic groups—natural breeds, hybrids, established breeds, and mutations. Natural breeds are those documented as being indigenous to a specific geographical region, where they appear to have reproduced consistently to a distinct physical type, color, and/or pattern by mating like to like. These include the Abyssinian, American Shorthair, British Shorthair, Chartreux, Egyptian Mau, Japanese Bobtail, Korat, Manx, Russian Blue, Siamese, and Singapura.

Hybrid breeds are the products of a cross between two or more natural breeds. These include the Bombay, Colorpoint Shorthair, Exotic Shorthair, Ocicat, Oriental Shorthair, Snowshoe, and Tonkinese.

Established breeds are those "manufactured" to conform to ideal characteristics that have been standardized from a specific color, pattern, or physical type originally unique to another breed's variants or the result of hybridization. Their genetic makeup is such that outcrosses (breeding with other breeds) are not required to maintain the breed. These include the Burmese and Havana Brown.

Mutations are breeds whose existence depends on a genetic idiosyncrasy that produces an unusual visible trait. These cats include the American Wirehair, Cornish Rex, Devon Rex, Scottish Fold, and Sphynx.

Natural Instincts

Although not an obvious attribute of the domestic cat, the hunting instinct is latent in most breeds, and they can, and will, hunt. Descendants of a North African wild cat, shorthair breeds are notable hunters, particularly the American Shorthair, which is really a pedigreed alley cat accustomed to hunting for its food amid garbage. An American Shorthair kitten stalking its toy mouse is simply reenacting the behavior of its forebears, the Old World working cats employed to control vermin. Ancestors of the British Shorthair and the Chartreux were around at the time of the Black (bubonic) Plague that devastated Europe in the 14th century and helped exterminate the rat population that carried the disease. Hunting and other instincts of shorthair cats have long been useful to man. In ancient times Siamese and their related ancestors were employed as guardians of great temples; today these breeds are still ready to alert their owners to visitors or intruders.

Appearance and Personality

Aesthetics are important in selecting a cat. Among the shorthairs choices range from angular, exquisite, racy-looking Siamese breeds to the plushy, dignified, chubby-cheeked Exotic Shorthair. Beyond appearance, each breed offers a different personality, and some are more people-oriented than others. The vocal Colorpoint Shorthair, for example, will engage in conversation with its owner, whereas an Exotic Shorthair will respond with little more than a sleepy blink. The extroverted Burmese will perform acrobatic feats even for strangers, while the more timid Russian Blue will probably hide. American and British Shorthairs remain impervious. The Tonkinese may act officious and fetch endlessly, while the Scottish Fold may crave nothing more than peace and quiet. Although the Korat and the Japanese Bobtail are both from the Far East, their behavior differs enough to demonstrate that geographic origin is not a reliable factor in judging a cat's personality.

Life-style

There is a shorthair cat for every life-style and preference. Some breeds need more living space than others, but this depends less on a cat's size than on its energy level. A pair of Singapuras will fit nicely into a studio apartment; a cat tree tucked into a corner is sufficient for this breed's exercise needs. The same apartment is probably just as comfortable for a pair of Exotics or big British Shorthairs because, despite their size, they are not especially active cats. On the other hand, the Tonkinese, Cornish Rex, and Devon Rex are acrobatic breeds that need an extended area—such as hallways and staircases—in which to play; the more sedentary breeds need only the length of an invitingly sunny windowsill.

Since shorthairs are inherently smart and need so little grooming, they are ideal companions for the elderly and the handicapped. Although one cat can live happily alone, it thrives best with the companionship of another cat, preferably one of the same breed, at least one of comparable vigor. An active breed's excess energy needs an outlet. A loner that depends exclusively on its owner for social and physical interaction is likely to become domineering and spoiled. When denied attention, the cat may cause continual mischief and become an unpleasant pest. A happy solution may be to keep two cats; each will occupy the other and make fewer demands on the owner.

Preferences
Some cat owners prefer shorthair breeds to longhairs simply because they require less grooming. Others are perhaps attracted to the raw power of the muscle and sinew visible beneath the gleaming, close-lying coat of a shorthair cat. Or perhaps it is a breed's history; the Abyssinian and the Egyptian Mau have an undeniable mystique that is partly rooted in their ancient Egyptian origins. Equally provocative are sleek, aristocratic breeds like the Siamese and the Oriental Shorthair, which reflect the sheer linear elegance of Far Eastern art. But no matter what governs the preference for shorthair breeds, devotees have a diverse array of colors, physiques, and compelling personalities from which to choose.

Abyssinian

Characteristics
Resembles a small
mountain lion
Regal appearance
Distinctive short,
ticked coat
Walks like a panther

Personality
Extremely affectionate, quiet, and highly intelligent. Very active and eager to participate in all family activities. Fearless, friendly, and extremely fast. A sun-worshiper, moving from window to window to bask. One of the most delightful pets.

Ideal Appearance
Medium-size. Overall impression is a colorful cat with a distinctly ticked coat. Must be touched to appreciate its beauty. Firm, muscular, well-balanced body. Intermediate build is svelte. Slightly rounded, wedge-shaped head with large ears and large, almond-shaped eyes. Fairly long tail, thick at base and tapering. Soft, silky coat is dense and resilient.

Colors
3 special breed colors: ruddy, red, and recently, blue. Ruddy, also known as normal in some associations, is most popular color. Ruddy is orange-brown, ticked with dark brown or black. Ears and tail are tipped with black; undersides of body and inside legs are even ruddy tone of orange-brown or burnt sienna, without ticking. Nose leather is tile-red, paw pads black or brown. Red is warm and glowing, ticked with chocolate-brown. Ears and tail are tipped with chocolate-brown. Nose leather and paw pads are pink. Blue is a warm soft blue-gray, distinctly ticked with various shades of slate-blue. Ears and tail tipped with slate-blue. Undersides and inside forelegs are warm, soft cream to beige. Nose leather is dark pink. Paw pads are mauve.

Potential Health Problems
Generally healthy. Certain lines may be susceptible to anesthetics. Inclined to have gingivitis (inflamed gums). Very rare cases of progressive retinal atrophy.

Care and Grooming
Like most shorthair breeds, the Abyssinian normally needs little grooming. However, a quick combing daily with a fine-toothed comb will help remove loose hair. Hand grooming—a hand-over-hand, firm stroking from head to tail—will remove dead hairs and give cat much pleasure. An occasional bath may be necessary if coat appears greasy. Nails need trimming regularly.

Kittens
Small litter, usually of 3 kittens. When born, kittens vary from dark orange with black patches to almost totally black. Color and ticking on coat, apparent at about 6 weeks, develop slowly. Some lines mature slowly and may not be fully ticked until 6 months or older. The Abyssinian is often likened to wine and cheese: it improves with age.
Kittens are strong and vigorous, climbing out of their basket before 4 weeks. Mother is very protective; enjoys young, playing with and chirping to them. Male is gentle with babies, allowing them to bite his tail and clamber all over him; will share in washing of young and will often stay with litter when the mother leaves.

Comment
Although many cat fanciers believe the Abyssinian is a direct descendant of the Sacred Cat of Egypt, the exact origin of the breed is obscure. Certainly there is a strong resemblance between the modern Abyssinian and the cat depicted in ancient Egyptian bronzes and paintings —the lithe, long body, large ears, and long tail. It also bears a striking similarity to small wild cats of North America. Most of the modern-day Abyssinians around the world had their beginnings in England. Several cats were taken back to England by soldiers returning from the Abyssinian War in 1868 (hence the breed name). The first registration of the breed appeared in English stud books in 1896, but there were still only 12 listed by 1905. The

first record of the breed in the United
States is of a pair in Boston, registered as
imported from England in 1909. But
few breeders were active until the 1930s,
when additional Abys were imported
from England. The war years sadly
depleted the English stock, but by the
late '40s, American breeders were hard at
work. Now it is not unusual for the Aby
to be the largest class of shorthair cats in
competition.

Recommendation

The Abyssiniàn is a most active and
affectionate cat. It needs and demands
freedom, does not take readily to small
spaces, and would probably be happier in
larger quarters. It needs lots of room,
preferably with access to the outdoors.
This intelligent breed can learn to
retrieve. It will readily walk on a leash
and harness (never a collar), especially if
it means an outing. Indoors, it likes
heights and will easily jump to the top
of a door or the refrigerator. Fearless,
friendly, and fond of water, it is often
found watching a dripping faucet or
playing in its water dish. The Aby is a
great family pet that gets along well
with dogs. It is often attractive to men
who previously thought they did not
like cats.

Plates 44, 45, 46, 47

American Shorthair

Characteristics
Powerful appearance
Big, broad, muscular
build
Wide, cheeky face
Short, hard coat

Personality
Gentle and compliant. Smart, agile athlete. Loud purrs, but tiny meows. Extremely quiet. Natural hunter. Has a dignity all its own. Independent.

Ideal Appearance
Medium to large. Heavy build indicates tremendous power. Well-knit, brawny body with broad chest, heavy shoulders, and thick hind legs. Oblong head on strong neck. Wide, cheeky face with wide-set ears allows plenty of space for markings. Round eyes. Open, sweet expression. Short, hard, dense coat; may be thicker in winter. Female smaller.

Colors
There are 34 recognized colors and patterns. Most common: classic tabby pattern, especially in silver, brown, red, or cameo; also common are black, blue, white, calico, shaded silver, or tortoiseshell. Other colors and patterns: red, cream, chinchilla, shell cameo, shaded cameo, black smoke, blue smoke, cameo smoke, tortoiseshell smoke; mackerel tabby pattern; patched tabby pattern in brown, blue, and silver; classic tabby pattern in blue or cream; dilute calico; blue-cream; bicolor; van bicolor; van calico; and van blue-cream and white. Chocolate, lavender, and Himalayan patterns are not acceptable. Nose leather and paw pads generally correspond to predominant color of cat, ranging from pink to black. Eyes may be gold, copper, green, hazel, blue, or odd-eyed, depending on coat color.

Potential Health Problems
Generally hardy breed.

Care and Grooming
This vigorous cat needs plenty of exercise. Can get lazy if not stimulated. Encourage it to race and wrestle with you. If you let your American Shorthair outside, an occasional bath might be required. Grooming with a rubber brush helps during the spring shedding season.

Kittens
Litters average 4 kittens. Compared to other breeds, kittens can be enormous, maturing quickly to 10-pound females, 14-pound males. Colors are usually identifiable at birth (except smokes). Appetites are voracious and frequent, never diminishing in the least through maturity. Owners should control their cat's diet to avoid obesity.

Comment
Probably our most familiar cats, American Shorthairs have patrolled our barns, fields, warehouses, and homes for pesky rodents ever since the first settlers arrived in America. Today they are still regarded as working cats.
With such a long American heritage, it is rather surprising that the first American Shorthairs—known simply as shorthairs—were not registered until the turn of the century and were in fact British imports, an orange tabby and a silver tabby. Then in 1904, Buster Brown, a male smoke of unknown American parents, was registered, thus opening the way for the American-bred stock.
Over the years this breed became known as the Domestic Shorthair; in 1966 the name American Shorthair was adopted. Nonpedigree cats are still called Domestics, and until January, 1985, these nonpedigreed Domestics were accepted by the CFA as foundation stock.

Recommendation
Extremely affectionate, the American Shorthair is a great lap cat, if you can bear the weight. It is easily disciplined and trained, and can learn to live with other pets, including birds. Most will accept roughhousing from children.

Plates 81, 82, 83, 84, 85

American Wirehair

Characteristics
Wiry coat
Well-muscled,
medium-size build
Round head

Personality
Quiet, reserved, and somewhat less receptive to strangers than the American Shorthair. Not especially vocal, although it will trill enthusiastically at feeding time. Playful kittens become affectionate, undemanding adults. Sweet expression.

Ideal Appearance
Medium-size to large. Wiry coat is breed's distinguishing characteristic. It should be springy, tight, and medium-long; individual hairs are crimped and wiry. Best coat is very dense, resilient, and coarse, with a curly appearance. Even hair between toes, on ears, and whiskers appears to curl. Overall well-muscled build similar to American Shorthair. Round head has large, open eyes.

Colors
This breed has 34 colors and patterns, the same as the American Shorthair. Black, white, blue, red, and tortoiseshell are the most popular. Other colors and patterns:. cream; chinchilla; shaded silver; shell or shaded cameo; black, blue, or cameo smoke; classic or mackerel tabby in silver, red, brown, blue, cream, or cameo; calico; dilute calico; blue-cream; bicolor; or any other color and pattern except chocolate, lavender, Himalayan patterns, or these combinations with white.
Most Wirehairs have gold eyes except for those cats that are white (with blue, gold, or odd eyes), chinchilla or shaded silver (with green or blue-green), or silver tabby (green or hazel).
Nose leather and paw pads correspond to predominant color of cat, ranging from pink to black.

Potential Health Problems
Generally hardy. Wiry coat easily damaged, but this probably does not affect health. No known genetic weaknesses.

Care and Grooming
Fragile, wiry coat is easily hurt. *Never* brush or comb it. Grooming would rip out the coat, leaving permanent patches. Do not allow a Wirehair outdoors, where coat could be damaged. Because crimped hairs tend to pick up every bit of lint and dust in the house, cat may need bathing approximately every 3 weeks. Excellent nutrition is a must to keep coat from becoming brittle and breaking.

Kittens
Usually 4 to 5 kittens per litter. Kittens resemble baby lambs. Depending upon parentage, half the litter will have curly coats, half straight coats. Straight coats may curl later, at around 8 weeks. Kittens are relaxed and enjoy attention.

Comment
The original litter of American Wirehairs was discovered in a barn in upstate New York in 1966. By the time the farmer decided to release the kittens to a local breeder, a weasel had killed all but one male. The kitten proved to be a mutation of the American Shorthair. Genetics revealed a semidominant gene that affects only the coat. One parent must be wirehaired to produce wirehair offspring. Today breeders still have little control over the desired coat other than breeding the best wirehair cats to American Shorthairs with thick, densely textured coats and hoping for the best. Results attained by breeding wirehairs to wirehairs are not as favorable. There are few American Wirehairs. They were accepted for CFA championship in 1978.

Recommendation
This laid-back cat is easy to get along with. A Wirehair is fine with children and other pets, adapting to a regular family schedule. Prospective owners should be prepared for careful screening.

Plates 79, 80

Bombay

Characteristics
Muscular body
Round head
Deep nose break
Semi-upright crouch
Black

Personality
Graceful, charming cat. Easygoing and friendly. Its slogan is, "Pet me, pet me!" Gets along well with other family pets and children. Playful, affectionate, and responsive, even with strangers. Enjoys family activity. Impish and sometimes silly.

Ideal Appearance
Medium-size. Incredibly muscular body feels like coiled steel springs wrapped around a lead core. Male is often quite a bit larger than female. Bombay and Burmese standards are almost identical, except the Bombay should not have a pug or snub face or ultracompact body. Rounded ears tilt slightly forward and deep nose break apparent in profile. Rounded head with broad forehead. Cat often assumes a semi-upright crouch, giving appearance of great agility.

Colors
Jet-black. Eyes are gold to copper. Nose leather and paw pads are black.

Potential Health Problems
Because of their Burmese heritage, certain lines of Bombay may have, or carry, genetic anomalies that are not immediately apparent. Have an experienced breeder check the pedigree of breeding cats for known carriers of heart, skull, spinal, and other possible defects that could be transmitted to offspring. Breeding Bombays should be considered only if the expert guidance of a trusted professional breeder is available.
Eyes may tear. Cat with deep nose break may have difficulty breathing. Basically healthy.

Care and Grooming
Little grooming necessary unless cat is being shown. An occasional bath with flea shampoo helps keep the coat glossy. Bombay loses its kitten coat at about 12 months; the old coat turns brownish and will not lie flat. Gently strip out the old coat with a rubber brush, taking care not to damage the new hair. May look somewhat motheaten for about a month.

Kittens
Average litter of 4 kittens. Those that look half naked will probably have the sleekest adult coats. Kittens are born lighter brown and darken with age. Body shape changes daily up to 8 weeks. Kittens should be lovingly handled from birth to make them comfortable with people. Little gluttons; need frequent feedings. Males can be sexually mature by 10 months (the bigger, the sooner). Almost all spray and, unless kept at stud, should be neutered.

Comment
The Bombay was produced in 1958 by crossing a sable Burmese with a black American Shorthair. The Cat Fanciers' Association accepted the breed for championship only in 1976, and few have been shown until recently. Thanks to its glossy black coat and bright, coppery eyes, the Bombay is known as the "patent-leather kid with the new penny eyes."

Recommendation
The Bombay adapts reasonably well to other animals and is usually courteous to guests. Fairly patient with children, some may be quite protective of their owners' infants. However, not all lines are as people-oriented as others. Check pedigrees and health records before buying a Bombay.

Plate 50

British Shorthair

Characteristics
Large head
Broad, deep body
Thick, single coat
Impressive appearance
Stands taller on legs
than American
Shorthair

Personality
Placid and easygoing. Sleeps a lot. Content to lie around the house. Can be aloof. Play gets left behind with kittenhood. Extremely dignified and gentle.

Ideal Appearance
Medium-size to large. More massive and taller than the American Shorthair. Massive head creates impression of bulk. In profile, forehead is rounded. Nose dips gently. Big, round eyes. Compact, deep body with broad chest and short neck. Described as a "ball on a box" planted squarely on sturdy, short to medium-length legs. Thick, single coat should be resilient and crisp to the touch. In its prime at 4 to 5 years.

Colors
Originally only in blue (called British Blue), there are now 18 recognized colors and patterns: white; black; blue; cream; black smoke; blue smoke; classic tabby or mackerel tabby pattern in silver, red, brown, blue, or cream; tortoiseshell; tortoiseshell and white; blue-cream; and bicolor. In addition, unique spotted tabby pattern. Most colors have gold or copper eyes. Nose leather and paw pads generally correspond to predominant color of cat, ranging from pink to black.

Potential Health Problems
No known genetic problems. Generally hardy.

Care and Grooming
Easy to groom. Most colors require only routine bathing except the white, which may need more frequent washing. To polish blue coat or tabby patterns, smooth on a very small amount of bay rum. Good muscle tone and healthy coat depend on a balanced diet.

Kittens
Average litter of 4 kittens. Even the runt is large. Pudgy kittens change weekly during the first 2 years. Although discerning a blue from a blue tabby may be difficult at first, most colors are readily identifiable. Kittens' coats are thick at birth. Blue coats plushier, due to inherent Persian genes. Kittens mature slowly; males may be well above 1 year old before exhibiting the mating instinct.

Comment
The oldest natural English breed, the British Shorthair probably traces its lineage back to the domestic cats of Roman times that later populated the streets of Europe and Britain. British Shorthairs, called European Shorthairs on the Continent, were among the first cats recognized as distinct breeds in the earliest English cat shows of the 1890s. Although the breed was known in America in 1900, it was not recognized by the Cat Fanciers' Association until the 1950s and qualified for championship status only in 1980.
Like its cousin the American Shorthair, the British Shorthair is still considered a working breed. However, the 2 breeds developed quite differently and today have distinct show standards. The British Shorthair has a larger head and a more compact, lower build than the American. At one time the British Shorthair breeders mated their cats to Persians to strengthen the body type, although this practice is no longer acceptable. Until recently, all British Shorthairs were imported, and many still are today.

Recommendation
It is easy to live with a British Shorthair. Nothing bothers it, and you will have to demand its attention. In complete incongruity to its size, the tiny voice is barely audible. Untemperamental, this breed is an ideal choice for busy households with little time to fuss.

Plates 86, 87, 88, 89, 90

Burmese

Characteristics
Compact, muscular torso
Rounded head
Small ears
Strong neck and shoulders
Glossy coat

Personality
A gleeful smart aleck and clever clown. Has complete repertoire of stunts from headstands to somersaults. Dance with hind legs called "Burmese shuffle" is characteristic of male before pouncing or prior to spraying. Can be bossy and stubborn. Demanding.

Ideal Appearance
Medium-size. Solid, short body. Build has become extreme in the CFA— compact and almost as cobby as Persian; not quite as extreme in other associations. Rounded head; no flat planes. Broad, short muzzle maintains rounded contours of head in profile, showing distinct nose break. Male tends to be jowly. (New look, called Eastern, has much flatter face and almost bulging forehead.) Small ears with rounded tips set well apart above broad forehead. Rounded, slightly Oriental eyes. Well-developed neck, especially in male. Powerful shoulders. Muscles ripple as cat moves. Short, sturdy legs. Tail tapers in proportion to body. Short, fine, glossy coat lies close to body.

Colors
Solid sable brown. Nose leather and paw pads brown. Eyes bright gold to yellow. The CFA also considers blue, champagne, and platinum to be Burmese. Other associations recognize these colors as the Malayan (see Malayan account).

Potential Health Problems
Prone to upper respiratory diseases as kittens, but maturity brings relief. Inbreeding for extreme domed head and pushed-in face has intensified heart defects and has led to mutative malformations of face and head and other abnormalities. Possible ocular dermoids and cardiomyopathy. Generally Burmese are healthy.

Care and Grooming
Little grooming necessary. Loose hair can be removed with the concave side of a rubber brush, then a damp hand. Polish with a chamois, terry washcloth, or piece of silk. Bathing is usually not necessary for pets but is recommended prior to shows. Too much dry food may produce mushy body instead of desired hard muscle tone.

Kittens
Litters of 6 kittens not uncommon. Very playful by 6 weeks. It is necessary to keep food dishes well supplied. Burmese are precocious, showing sexual interest at about 5 months.

Comment
Although solid brown cats resembling the Burmese are mentioned in Siam's *Cat-Book Poems* of A.D. 1350, the Burmese breed as we know it was developed in the United States in the 1930s as the result of one man's fascination with a single cat. Dr. Joseph Thompson's little brown female from Burma, Wong Mau, was the first of her kind in the United States. When Wong Mau was bred to her closest Malayan relative, the Siamese, she herself proved to be a hybrid, probably the equivalent of the present-day Tonkinese. This was evident because she produced kittens with Siamese coloring, dark brown kittens, and intermediate kittens. The solid brown kittens were retained for Dr. Thompson's breeding program, and the Burmese was registered with the Cat Fanciers' Association in 1936. Nearly every breeder in America can trace the pedigree of their Burmese to Wong Mau.

Recommendation
Most Burmese have a sweet disposition combined with a delightful sense of humor. A Burmese expects rewards; but you'll enjoy the give and take as much as it does. Happy, active cats with fairly soft voices, they are superb additions to the family.

Plate 51

Chartreux

Characteristics
Massive, robust cat
Wide forehead
Narrow muzzle
Slight break in nose
Appears to smile
Soft, dense blue coat

Personality
Warm and friendly. Smiles a lot. Loves children and large dogs. This hefty, muscular cat knows its own strength; gentle with people, it can be tough on rodents—a great mouser. Often perches on sunny windowsills. Rarely heard, except for occasional deep purrs.

Ideal Appearance
Large. Massive, robust cat with broad chest and powerful hind legs. Males, usually 10 to 14 pounds; females, 6 to 9 pounds. Build similar to British Shorthair except does not have round head. Broad head has wide forehead, extremely full cheeks, and narrow, but not pointed, muzzle. Short, straight nose with only slight break below eyes. Good jaws indicate hunting origins. Cat appears to smile; an angry look is considered a show penalty. Dense, plush, medium-length coat should be as soft as rabbit fur.

Colors
Blue; any shade acceptable. Some standards specify silvery overtones or highlights. Eyes are gold to copper. Nose leather and paw pads are blue.

Potential Health Problems
No known genetic defects. Generally an extraordinarily healthy breed.

Care and Grooming
Little grooming required, but cat loves a good brushing, either with a natural bristle brush or even a wire brush. If allowed outdoors, cat may need bathing periodically. A generous, balanced diet and vitamins are recommended for this robust eater. Males rarely spray, are very clean, and are generally nonaggressive.

Kittens
Average of 2 kittens per litter. Kittens are fat, sturdy, and slow to wean. They will eat everything in sight while continuing to nurse for at least 2 months. Extremely playful and responsive, kittens are great jumpers, mock hunters.

Comment
Among the oldest natural breeds, the Chartreux developed rather mysteriously centuries ago in France. It is believed that the breed was brought from the Cape of Good Hope to France by the Carthusian monks famous for their Chartreuse liqueur. Whether the monks gave the cats they bred the name Chartreux or people associated them with the monastery is unknown. By the 18th century, however, this handsome blue cat is documented by both Linnaeus and Buffon in their writings. Two centuries earlier the French poet du Bellay had described similar blue-gray cats, possibly Chartreux, and acclaimed their ability as ratters.

During World War II, the number of Chartreux had so declined in France that many were crossed with other breeds, leaving only a few pedigree lines intact. Some of these purebred Chartreux were brought to the United States. Eventually enough cats were produced to gain the breed recognition by several associations. Although the breed is still not recognized for show by the Cat Fanciers' Association, it may be registered. The CFA proposed standard is almost identical to that for the British Shorthair.

Recommendation
Some Chartreux will demand attention by batting with their paws; most quietly await your notice. Extremely awkward in confined spaces, this cat needs room to bound and demonstrate its innate coordination. The Chartreux loves heights and deftly leaps from the floor to the top of the refrigerator for an overview. Easy to train, it is an excellent choice for households with young children and a dog.

Plate 49

Colorpoint Shorthair

Characteristics
Resembles Siamese
Svelte, dainty look
Elongated, muscular body
Wedge-shaped head
Pointed pattern

Personality
More than just a companion or a pet. Count the Colorpoint among your most intelligent, compassionate, feeling friends. Always where you are, it will offer suggestions and argue a point vociferously. Unpredictable. A real cuddler.

Ideal Appearance
Medium-size. Colorpoints are genetically Siamese and are categorized as new color Siamese in every association except the CFA. Elongated, angular body with wedge-shaped head. A superb construction of muscle and sinew wrapped around exquisite bones. Tight, close coat.

Colors
Point colors: red, cream, seal tortie, chocolate tortie, blue-cream, or lilac-cream; also lynx-point patterns in seal, chocolate, blue, lilac, or red. Eyes are vivid blue. Nose leather and paw pads harmonize with coat color and range from pink to seal-brown. Recognized by several other associations in all Siamese and all Oriental Shorthair point-restricted categories.

Potential Health Problems
Susceptible to upper respiratory illnesses as kittens but, once recovered, have incredibly strong constitution. Sensitive to anesthetics; necessary surgical procedures should be undertaken with an anesthetic over which a veterinarian has ideal control. Some lines may carry heart defects or cleft palates. Usually healthy.

Care and Grooming
Little special grooming necessary. A high-protein, balanced diet, vitamins, and jumping space are essential.

Kittens
Litter of 2 to 8 kittens. At birth, kittens look like tiny, pink, nearly nude white mice. Royal blue eyes open in about a week. Huge ears and long, skinny tails are out of proportion to bodies. Color first shows at tips of ears and spine of tail. Can be very stubborn about eating. Phenomenal climbers, kittens are easily taught to use ceiling-height scratching post, not drapes.

Comment
Though documented earlier, Colorpoint Shorthair breeding programs were really established in England in 1947–48 and then later in America. Standard-color Siamese, with seal, blue, chocolate, or lilac points, were bred to red cats—probably domestics, but perhaps also Abyssinians—producing tortoiseshell-pattern-pointed Siamese. When these cats, in turn, were bred to one another and then their progeny back to standard-color Siamese, the results were cats with red points, cream points, and tortie points, as well as the standard-color-pointed offspring. The original crosses produced cats that were later deliberately bred for solid and full-color patterns and are now called Oriental Shorthairs in the United States. The pointed kittens in the new colors were recognized in England as Colorpoint Shorthairs or Siamese, but it took much longer for the breed to be accepted in the United States. In the 1960s, lynx points were introduced in the same manner. It actually took more than 25 years, until 1974, for the Colorpoint Shorthair to achieve CFA championship status in America. Because Siamese breeders did not want to recognize any colors beyond the classic 4 point colors, the new colors were given a separate breed identity.

Recommendation
Audacious, demanding, vocal, arrogant, and full of nonsense, Colorpoints are also passionately loving and intelligent. The Colorpoint Shorthair is always on stage.

Plates 61, 62, 63, 64

Cornish Rex

Characteristics
Long, narrow head
with big, flared ears
Roman nose
Look of surprise
Soft, velvety coat
Arched body

Personality
Chic-looking, but really a lap cat.
Properly raised, it enjoys handling and
projects warmth. Generally talkative;
voice is high-pitched and somewhat like
Siamese but not as piercing. Excellent
with children. Playful.

Ideal Appearance
Small to medium-size. Unusual curved
appearance and wavy, rippling, plushy
coat. Long, narrow head has a rounded
forehead over a prominent Roman nose.
Large, flared, erect ears set high on head
and oval eyes give cat a look of surprise.
Crinkled whiskers and eyebrows. Body
arches like that of a greyhound, torso is
tucked up at waist. Cat appears angular
but is really a complexity of curves:
profile curves in 2 convex arches. Long,
muscular legs support arched body. Coat
is fuller than that of Devon Rex; has
tight, close wave and looks and feels like
cut velvet. Coat lacks guard hairs.

Colors
There are 28 recognized colors and
patterns: white; black; blue; red; cream;
chinchilla; shaded silver; black smoke;
blue smoke; classic tabby or mackerel
tabby patterns in silver, red, brown,
blue, or cream; patched tabby patterns in
brown, blue, or silver; tortoiseshell,
calico, van calico, dilute calico, blue-
cream, van blue-cream and white,
bicolor, and van bicolor. Most have gold
eyes. Lavender, chocolate, or pointed
patterns, called Si-Rex, are not accepted
in most associations.

Potential Health Problems
Coat is fragile and lacks guard hairs. Cat
must be kept warm and protected from
extreme heat and cold.

Care and Grooming
Curly coat is delicate and easily
damaged, since it lacks guard hairs. Do
not allow direct contact with heat
sources or use any abrasives. Brush
occasionally with soft brush, avoiding
friction or overbrushing, which will
result in bald spots. Normal body
temperature is 1 degree higher than
other breeds, which can confuse
veterinarians who are unfamiliar with the
breed. Higher metabolism results in
huge appetites; food is rapidly burned
off. Do not let cats overeat or they will
become fat. Cornish Rex is not an
outdoor cat.

Kittens
Small litters of 3 to 4 kittens. Colors
recognizable at birth. Kittens are the size
of mice and look like little curly bears
(they even have curly whiskers). Very
playful, growing into very active
creatures.

Comment
Born in Cornwall, England, in 1950, a
cat named Kallibunker became the
foundation cat of the first Rex breeding
program. Of domestic parents,
Kallibunker was bred back to its mother.
A second spontaneous mutation had
occurred in Germany to produce the
Lammchen lines, which proved to be the
same mutation as the Cornish Rex.
Imported to America in 1960, the Rex
was soon established as a championship
breed in most associations. In 1979, the
Cat Fanciers' Association established the
Cornish Rex as distinct from the Devon
Rex, which is an entirely different
natural mutation: the two do not
produce curly or wavy-coated offspring.

Recommendation
While the Cornish Rex is very
affectionate, not everyone wants to hug
this highly stylized cat. This is a breed
for avant-garde tastes. Because the Rex
lacks guard hairs, it produces little
dander, and thus may be one of the few
breeds people allergic to cats can
tolerate. Extroverted and persistently
inquisitive, this energetic cat finds
children and pets good company.

Plates 73, 74, 75, 76

Devon Rex

Characteristics
Short, wedge-shaped head
Big, low-set ears
Body not arched
Fuzzier, less curly coat than that of Cornish Rex

Personality
Chatty, but not as talkative as the Siamese or even the Cornish Rex. Prefers company of people to that of other animals. Has several doglike traits, including retrieving. Excellent climber.

Ideal Appearance
Medium-size. Resembles a pixie with large eyes and ears. Wavy coat longer, fuzzier, less curly than coat of Cornish Rex; feels like suede or brushed corduroy. Underparts may be covered with down. Short, wedge-shaped face with pronounced cheekbones, short nose, and prominent whisker pads. Crinkled whiskers and eyebrows. Large, wide-based ears, set low on head, are an outstanding characteristic; ears may be tufted. Slender neck. Slender, muscular body with broad chest and long legs. Body not arched like that of Cornish Rex. More delicately sculptured than Cornish Rex.

Colors
Accepted in nearly all colors appropriate to American Shorthairs and British Shorthairs. Solid white with gold eyes shown most often. Other solid colors: black, blue, red, cream, chinchilla; shaded pattern; smoke pattern; classic tabby, mackerel tabby, or spotted tabby pattern in silver, brown, blue, red, or cream; patched tabby pattern; tortoiseshell; blue-cream; and white spotting patterns. Most have gold eyes. Nose leather and paw pads harmonize with coat color and range from pink to blue to black. Lavender, chocolate, and Himalayan patterns shown only in Any Other Variety class.

Potential Health Problems
Coat cannot tolerate physical duress. Cat must be kept warm and not exposed to extremes of temperature.

Care and Grooming
Like the Cornish Rex, the Devon Rex needs a high-fat diet to supplement high metabolism. Also needs a balanced diet sufficient in protein. Grooming should be done very carefully to avoid friction or overbrushing, which will cause bald spots. The best way to groom a Devon is with your hands—and it loves every minute of it! Devons exude warmth, the result of a higher than normal body temperature.

Kittens
Usually 3 to 5 kittens per litter. Bare patches not uncommon on kittens and young adults. Tiny, mouselike infants may be hairless. Kittens are relatively small; even males are dainty.

Comment
Devons are descended from a cat called Kirlee, the result of mating a feral domestic to a cared-for stray. Kirlee was given to a breeder in the neighboring English county of Cornwall, where another Rex—Kallibunker—had appeared 10 years earlier, in 1950. But when Kirlee was mated to Kallibunker, their offspring had only straight coats. Further efforts proved that 2 different Rex genes were involved, Cornish and Devon, and that they would not mix. In fact, they produced 2 distinctly different types of coat and even different physical characteristics. The 2 breeds have been bred and registered separately since the second (Devon) Rex gene was ascertained, except in the CFA. Devons were first registered as such in the CFA in 1979.

Recommendation
Those who prize the unique will appreciate Devon Rexes. Their impish faces match their charm. While not fragile, they prefer a light touch and much attention. They should be protected from extremes of weather.

Plates 77, 78

Egyptian Mau

Characteristics
Distinct spot pattern
Gooseberry-green eyes
Fine, silky coat
Muscular physique

Personality
Somewhat reserved; can be quite aloof with strangers. Character depends considerably on bloodlines and rearing environment. Some dislike handling and react adversely; others obviously enjoy limelight and respond to handling with pleasure. Quiet, with low, melodious voice.

Ideal Appearance
Medium-size. Most important characteristic is spotted pattern; this is the only naturally spotted domestic breed. Head is gently contoured wedge. Nose even in breadth from forehead to tip. Ears, sometimes tufted, are broad at base, upstanding. Eyes almond-shaped but not Oriental. Well-balanced body with hind legs longer than front legs, giving impression that cat is on tiptoes when standing upright. Coat is fine, silky, short, dense, and resilient, suited for showing off spotted pattern. Each hair is long enough for 2 or more bands of darker ticking separated by lighter banding.

Colors
The spotted pattern applies to all colors: silver, bronze, or smoke. Contrast between markings and ground color is critical. Eyes are gooseberry-green. Color of nose leather and paw pads according to coat color; brick-red to black. Marking the forehead are frown lines and an M (or scarab), lines continuing over head and back of neck, breaking into spots along the spine. Spots blend over haunches, forming a dorsal stripe, which continues down the tail. Tail is ringed, with a dark tip. Color on tail, paws, necklaces dense to roots. Mascara lines contour eyes and cheeks, with at least one unbroken necklace encircling the neck and chest. Front legs heavily barred. Front and back shoulders and upper hind legs bear transitional markings. Underside of body shows dark buttons against a lighter ground color.

Both sides of the Mau's torso bear random spotting, varying in size and shape but at least clearly delineated rosettes (not broken stripes).

Potential Health Problems
Generally healthy breed.

Care and Grooming
Normal, routine brushing. Periodic baths if allowed outside. Balanced diet.

Kittens
Litters average 4 husky kittens, which develop slowly. Spotted at birth, except smokes, which take about 6 weeks to identify. Eye color is a phenomenon: when kitten is happy, eyes get greener; if disturbed, color becomes amber. Eyes stabilize green at about 2 years. Kittens not fussy about eating but not interested until about 6 weeks. Both sexes said to be good parents.

Comment
Mau is the Egyptian word for "cat." This cat's alert, muscular physique is inherited from its hunting ancestors along the Nile. Prowling in high grass, it moves like a cheetah or a small leopard. Egyptian origins are documented by papyrus scrolls and temple paintings dating from 1400 B.C. Maus were imported to the United States in 1953. Though shown in Europe and Canada for years, it was not until 1978 that they became popular, the Cat Fanciers' Association recognizing them first. Maus are now in championship in all American associations, but there are still relatively few shown.

Recommendation
Some lines are excitable and unpredictable. Most are great pets, patient with children, and very affectionate within the family. They are not fond of strangers.

Plate 70

Exotic Shorthair

Characteristics
Large, round head
Short nose
Big, round, wide-set eyes
Compact build
Short legs
Dense, plush coat

Personality
Fairly placid. Unruffled manner makes it good with children. Acts like Persian yet is easy to groom. Basically quiet and content. Might jump as high as the bed to get comfortable.

Ideal Appearance
Medium-size to large. Compact, cobby build; resembles Persian except for short hair, and show standard is nearly identical. Massive, round head with a tremendous skull and small, rounded ears. Large, round eyes set far apart; short, snub nose with deep break between full cheeks. Jaws are broad and short, but powerful. Compact body with expansive chest. Stands low on short legs. Short tail in proportion to body. Dense, plush, soft, medium-length coat stands out from body more from thickness than from length. Double coat feels like soft, cottony shearling.

Colors
Same as Persian except solid colors of lavender and chocolate not allowed. (Basically same as American Shorthair with Persian additions.) White; black; blue; red; cream; chinchilla; shaded silver; chinchilla golden, shaded golden; shell cameo, shaded cameo; shell tortoiseshell, shaded tortoiseshell; black smoke, blue smoke, cameo smoke, smoke tortoiseshell; classic or mackerel tabby pattern in silver, red, brown, blue, cream, or cameo; patched tabby pattern in brown, blue, or silver; tortoiseshell; calico; dilute calico; blue-cream; bicolor, van bicolor, van calico, and van blue-cream and white. Most have copper eyes, but eye color and color of nose leather and paw pads correspond to predominant color of coat.

Potential Health Problems
Watch for malformed jaws and teeth, and breathing problems, typical of Persians. Foreshortened face can result in difficulty with chewing, eyes tearing,

and chronic sinus problems. Cat should not snort when it breathes, nor should it breathe through its mouth. Queens may need help (manual or surgical) delivering kittens, due to their huge skulls.

Care and Grooming
Easy to groom, requiring only routine daily brushing to remove dead hairs. Provide plenty of nutritious food; diet contributes to a healthy coat. Cat exercises itself.

Kittens
Litters average 4 kittens, with long or short coats. Colors are fairly obvious at birth, but plushy coat develops gradually, usually visible by 4 to 6 weeks. The softer the coat, the greater the probability of long hair. Kittens are chunky, with faces flattening out and ears becoming erect by 4 to 5 months. Physical growth is quick, but sexual maturity takes 2 to 4 years.

Comment
Often described as a shorthair Persian, the Exotic Shorthair was developed by crossing Persians with American Shorthairs. Like the Persian, the Exotic has a compact, short-legged build with a short, pushed-in face. From the American Shorthair it gained the shorter coat, which is, however, much thicker and somewhat longer than that of other shorthair breeds. In the early years, Burmese and British Shorthairs were also used for breeding, but since 1968 these 2 types have not been allowed. The Exotic Shorthair has been recognized by the CFA since 1966.

Recommendation
A highly practical breed for those who want the Persian type with a sweet facial expression but without the grooming headache. This undemanding cat is an ideal pet.

Plates 42, 93, 94, 95, 96, 97, 98

Havana Brown

Characteristics
Protruding, boxy
muzzle
Dark brown
Vivid green eyes
Brown whiskers
Lacks hair on ears
Long legs

Personality
Pixieish, people-oriented cat. Needs to be with its owner, and hates to be ignored. Affectionate. Insists on intimacy. Less vocal than Siamese or Oriental Shorthair.

Ideal Appearance
Medium-size. Female averages weight of 6 to 7 pounds; males, 8 to 9 pounds. Distinctive rectangular muzzle and mahogany color. Head slightly longer than it is wide. Muzzle has a break on either side of whisker pads, which makes jowls seem to extend. Muzzle protrudes squarely, accented by well-developed chin. Distinct stop at eyes. Very large, erect ears, pricked slightly forward, give intense look. Little hair on inside or outside of ears. Bare triangle on chin, below lower lip. Tail in proportion to body. Long legs make cat appear tall for its length. Short to medium-length coat; flat but not slick.

Colors
Dark brown. Has a reddish burnt sienna or mahogany cast. Nose leather is rosy brown. Paw pads rosy pink-brown. Brown whiskers. Vivid green eyes.

Potential Health Problems
No known genetic defects. Quite hardy.

Care and Grooming
Daily grooming unnecessary. Once a week brush coat gently with rubber brush to remove dead hairs. Polish and shine coat by rubbing with bare hands or chamois. Occasional bath keeps coat healthy. Cat is very oral, washing itself and companions frequently. Havana Brown breeders feed their cats a balanced diet, adding oil to generate coat luster.

Kittens
Usually 3 to 4 in litter. Born lighter shade of brown, often with ghost tabby markings that disappear later. Kittens look like bats because of large ears and pink noses. Out of box at 3 weeks; responding to human voice even before opening eyes. Males mature very early; physical prime is 2 years. Males are chauvinists; kitten-rearing is strictly for the females.

Comment
The first Havana Brown was registered in England in 1954, after years of selective breeding that began by crossing a black Domestic Shorthair cat with a seal-point Siamese carrying the brown gene. The result, a solid-colored brown cat, was developed into 2 separate breeds—the chestnut Oriental Shorthair (bred for its Siamese body type) and the Havana Brown (bred for its own unique characteristics). The breed became known as the Havana after a rabbit breed of the same color. Contemporary Havanas retain the characteristics of the original Havanas imported into this country. Despite their early hybrid origins, today only the cats bred like to like produce 100 percent Havana Browns. Accepted for championship in the CFA in 1960, Havana Browns are still rarely seen in show rings.

Recommendation
The Havana Brown is ideal for the person who wants a constant companion. Shoulders are its favorite perch. Friends are greeted with a raised paw. This breed's moods fluctuate from reserved to vivacious. Highly adaptable, the Havana will entertain itself with cardboard boxes and paper bags, and is happiest playing with other feline companions. Future owners beware: you do not own a Havana; it owns you.

Plate 69

Japanese Bobtail

Characteristics
Trim, medium body
Bobtail
High cheekbones
Slanted eyes
Triangular head
Deeply angulated
hind legs

Personality
Affectionate and generally sweet-tempered. Enjoys supervising household chores and baby-sitting. Well-defined sense of family life. Agile. Not particularly vocal.

Ideal Appearance
Medium-size to large. Bobbed tail is outstanding characteristic of breed. Tail is multikinked or may form a corkscrew. Some Bobtails have straight stub, unacceptable for show. Thicker fur on tail forms pompom like a rabbit's tail. Tail carried erect. Head forms almost perfect equilateral triangle. High cheekbones. Slanted, luminous eyes. Large, upright ears, pricked forward, not flared. Well-muscled body, lean and straight. Hind legs disproportionately tall but deeply angulated so that standing cat appears to be level. Silky, medium-length coat.

Colors
Preferred color and pattern is a tricolored cat, called *mi-ke* (pronounced mee-kay), which means "three fur" in Japanese. Most dramatic and popular mi-ke is red, black, and white calico pattern. Bicolors of black and white or red and white are next in preference. In both bi- and tricolors, any color may dominate as long as patches of color are bold, contrasting vividly with white ground. Also solid white, red, or black; tortoiseshell pattern in black, red, and cream. There are 23 possible color combinations accepted for show. Siamese pattern or unpatterned ticked coloring are not acceptable. Eyes may be gold, green, blue; or white cats may have 1 blue and 1 gold eye. Nose leather and paw pads coordinate with dominant coat color.

Potential Health Problems
Sensitive tail easily injured; structure is rigid bone. Generally healthy.

Care and Grooming
Do not manipulate tail: the acute pain that may result can cause irreparable physical and psychological harm. Protect cat from mishandling by children. If hurt once, the cat will always be wary of caresses to the degree that it may not permit handling at all. Brush occasionally. Predominantly white cats may need periodic bathing. Provide normal feline diet.

Kittens
Usually a litter of 4 kittens. Inordinately large at birth, especially heads and feet. Colors immediately apparent. At birth, appearance of cheekbones, eye slant, and characteristic tail determine future quality. Kittens are vigorous, hale, hearty adventurers.

Comment
Since antiquity, Japanese Bobtails, the domestic cats of Japan, have been documented in paintings, wood carvings, and statues, and on building façades. The Japanese traditionally regard the tricolored mi-ke cats as fortunate. Replicas of mi-ke cats, right paw raised in greeting, are a symbol of welcome and good luck. An American living in Japan brought the first Bobtail cats to the United States. Japanese interest in the breed grew only after American judges visiting a Japanese cat show in 1963 admired the Bobtails. They are known affectionately as Bobs. The breed gained CFA recognition in 1978.

Recommendation
A Bobtail usually holds up its end of a conversation, responding to humans in an expressive, chirpy little voice. It will often hum for its owner and will hint at a game of fetch by carrying an object around in its mouth. Unlike most cats, the Bobtail enjoys frolicking in water.

Plates 107, 108

Korat

Characteristics
Silver-blue coat with
halo effect
Luminous eyes
Heart-shaped face
Trim, muscular body

Personality
Intelligent and active. Soft-spoken.
Receptive to human overtures. Sense of
responsibility to family. The Korat
(pronounced koh-raht) has a strong sense
of time and place. Original imports
retain a sweetness not always inherited in
Western breeding. Not especially vocal.

Ideal Appearance
Medium-size. Heart-shaped head with
good breadth between and across eyes.
Eyebrow ridges form upper curves of
heart, and sides of face gently curve to
chin to complete shape. Eyes very large,
slanted, luminous; appear oversize in
proportion to face. Rounded when open,
but slant apparent when closed. Slight
nose stop with lionlike downward curve
to leather. Ears rounded at tip, widely
flared at base, set high on head.
Semicobby body is muscular and supple,
with look of tension. Back carried in
curve. Short to medium-length coat is
fine and glossy and lies close to body.
Coat over spine may break as cat moves.
Males should look like fighters, females
dainty.

Colors
Silver-blue ground tipped with silver,
the more silver the better; sheen or halo
effect most apparent where coat is
shortest. Nose leather and lips dark blue
or lavender. Paw pads range from dark
blue to lavender with pinkish tinge.
Luminous green eyes preferred, amber to
amber-green acceptable; eye color may
take 2 to 4 years to mature.

Potential Health Problems
Prone to upper respiratory viruses;
routine vaccinations mandatory. Watch
for shot reactions. Generally healthy.

Care and Grooming
Daily brushing and vitamin-
supplemented, balanced feline diet help
keep coat in prime condition. When cat
is out of shape, coat loses halo effect.
Give cat opportunity for exercise,
especially jumping and climbing, to
keep body muscular. Pair of Korats will
exercise each other.

Kittens
Generally 4 to 5 kittens in litter, but
may be many more. Young kittens
especially prone to viruses. Very playful,
active, extremely dependent on humans.
Need extra-loving environment. Adult
cats love babies, watch over and play
with youngsters. Males extremely
aggressive; reputation as street fighters in
native Thailand reflected in kittens'
warriorlike activity.

Comment
Beloved for centuries in its native
Thailand, the Korat is depicted in *The
Cat-Book Poems* dating from A.D. 1350 to
1767 and preserved in Bangkok's
National Library. Among the 17 Good
Luck cats pictured is the Si-Sawat,
known in this country as the Korat,
whose "hairs are smooth with roots like
clouds and tips like silver," and whose
"eyes shine like dewdrops on a lotus
leaf."
The Korat is rare even in Thailand,
where ownership is restricted by the
government. The first record of
registration in the United States dates
from 1959, when 2 Korats, named Nara
and Darra, arrived in Oregon. These
silver-blue cats with the Thai heritage
were accepted for CFA championship in
1966.

Recommendation
Western cats inherit some but not all the
sweetness of imported Korats. It is
important to find a breeder who selects
for temperament traits as well as health
and beauty. The Korat is reticent with
strangers but enjoys the close
companionship of its owner. Protective
of family members, Korats have been
known to alert them in emergencies.
This is a street-smart indoor pet.

Plate 92

Malayan

Characteristics
Medium-size
Gives impression of power
Strong neck and shoulders

Personality
Malayan is an other-color Burmese, so it is equally lively, demanding, and sometimes bossy. Can be quite assertive. Likes to play games. Smart, with sense of humor.

Ideal Appearance
Medium-size. Solid, compact build. Strong neck and shoulders. Physical conformation is same as for Burmese. Most associations consider Malayan same breed in different colors. According to the CFA, the Malayan is a division of Burmese; overall standard applies, but colors are separated. Coat texture of blues is coarser, due to structure of blue hair.

Colors
Blue, champagne, or platinum are the accepted colors in the United States. In other parts of the world, many other colors are recognized. Nose leather and paw pads on champagnes are pink to cinnamon; on blues, blue; on platinums, pink. Eyes are brilliant gold.

Potential Health Problems
Some upper respiratory disease in kittens; heart and possibly other defects due to inbreeding. Otherwise generally healthy.

Care and Grooming
Little grooming needed. Coat benefits from occasional rubdown with chamois or soft cloth. Blues may require higher fat content in food to help offset rougher coat quality. A good conditioner also helps.

Kittens
Litters of about 6 kittens. Genetic anomalies common to Burmese also exist in Malayans, so selective breeding is crucial. Dark mask is more common among lighter colors: champagne kittens, especially, take longer to lose markings, if they ever do. Willful, precocious, and energetic, kittens will scramble up to your shoulder. Keep their nails clipped.

Comment
At present, the Cat Fanciers' Association considers the Malayan a division of the Burmese breed, with its own color class. Although its status has shifted back and forth over the years, this cat is Burmese by ancestry. The fact that Wong Mau, first of the Burmese line, was herself a hybrid, and that Siamese were used in early breeding programs, naturally meant that colors other than sable existed in the Burmese gene pool. These colors were rejected by purist breeders who felt that Burmese meant "brown." However, a well-known breeder produced a champagne cat that was as distinct a type as any sable-colored Burmese being shown. The result, with the happy cooperation of other fanciers who had long been working for recognition of other-color Burmese, was acceptance in the Cat Fanciers' Association. The CFA stipulated that the cats be called Malayans to distinguish them from the sables. Although some purists believed that the new colors would contaminate the pure brown lines, documentation shows that, if a cat's lineage is explored through enough generations, blue, champagne, and platinum cats exist somewhere in every Burmese pedigree. In fact, the line that produced the first champagne grand champion had never before produced anything but sables.

Recommendation
Malayans are fun and outstanding companions. They are very easy to live with, as long as you accept their air of feline superiority. Blues may be more reserved than other colors.

Plates 52, 53, 54

Manx

Characteristics
Complete taillessness
desirable for show
Overall impression of
roundness
Massive rump
Longer hind legs
Double coat

Personality
A devilish, stubborn clown. Lots of
bluster. Lively and intelligent, very
owner-oriented. Needs discipline, easily
trained. Not very vocal.

Ideal Appearance
Medium-size but surprisingly heavy.
Distinctive characteristic is taillessness.
Perfect specimen, called rumpy, has
dimple where tail should be. Not for
show: stumpy—with short tail stump—
and longy—with complete tail present.
Solid, compact cat. Gives overall
impression of roundness. Round head
and muzzle, prominent cheeks. Face is
full, males heavily jowled. Whisker
break, fat whisker pads, slight nose dip
Medium-size ears with rounded tips,
wide at base; few hairs inside ears.
Round eyes. Thick neck. Short back
arches from shoulders to round rump and
is unique to Manx. Rump considerably
higher than shoulders. Short front legs,
long hind legs, thick and sturdy. Deep
flanks, bulging thighs. Trunk like a
barrel. Double coat. Plush, thick,
cottony undercoat with harder, glossy
topcoat.

Colors
Solid white, black, blue, red, cream, or
chinchilla; shaded silver, black smoke, or
blue smoke; classic or mackerel tabby
pattern in silver, red, brown, blue, or
cream; patched tabby pattern in brown,
blue, or silver; tortoiseshell, calico,
dilute calico, blue-cream, or bicolor.
Color and pattern not very important for
show points. Most Manxes have copper
eyes, but depending on coat color, eyes
may also be green, blue-green, or hazel;
white cats may have deep blue, copper,
or odd eyes. Nose leather and paw pads
range from pink to blue to black.

Potential Health Problems
Not a breed for the novice cat fancier.
The Manx carries a lethal gene: lack of
tail is a genetic defect indicating spinal
deformities (spina bifida) and cartilage
weaknesses. These may affect the legs
and neck, causing paralysis. A Manx
should be able to stand, walk, run, and
climb normally. A "bunny hop" gait is a
trait but may indicate problems.

Care and Grooming
Big appetite for big cat; needs balanced
feline nutrition. Brush thick coat often,
especially during "shaggy" winter
months. Bathe only if cat gets dirty.

Kittens
Very small litters; high proportion of
stillbirths and malformations. Surviving
kittens are chunky baby bears, tough,
outgoing, and affectionate.

Comment
Much legend surrounds the Manx, whose
homeland is the Isle of Man, between
England and Ireland. Stories of how they
got there and why they have no tails
involve considerable fantasy and
imagination. Some believe that the Manx
may have come from ancient Japan,
reaching Britain via Phoenician traders;
others speculate that it swam ashore from
the wreck of a Spanish Armada fleet ship
returning from a voyage to the Middle
East. The Manx's taillessness has long
been the subject of myth: one such story
has it that the cat was the last animal to
board the Ark, and Noah slammed the
door on its tail. In fact, the tailless Manx
is a genetic mutation. It is among the
earliest of breeds to have been registered
in Europe, Great Britain, and North
America.

Recommendation
An affectionate, unique companion, the
Manx should be purchased with caution
and then enjoyed for its buoyant spirit.
A good Manx is alert, intelligent,
healthy, and powerful. It leans toward
one-on-one relationships. Stumpies and
longies are best for pets.

Plates 101, 102, 103, 104, 105

Ocicat

Characteristics
Polka-dot pattern
Males extremely large
Wild appearance
Athletic build

Personality
Friendly, sweet temperament. Gentle. Sunny disposition. Moderately vocal. Despite its resemblance to a wild cat, quite tame and subdued.

Ideal Appearance
Females medium-size, males very large, 12 to 15 pounds. Wild, feral appearance is characteristic, as is coat patterned with round polka dots. Alert, athletic, shows great vitality. Modified oval head rises in a smooth curve from bridge of nose to forehead. Almond-shaped eyes angle downward toward broad nose. Moderately large, sometimes tufted ears at corners of egg-shaped face. Muscular body is rather long, lithe, and sleek. Medium-long legs proportionate to body. Slightly tapered tail is fairly long. Coat is fine, satiny, close-lying.

Colors
Spotted pattern in 8 colors. Hairs, except tip of dark tail, show bands of color in agouti pattern. Where bands fall together, a dot is formed. Colors are silver with black dots; blue with slate-blue dots; tawny (buff or ruddy) with black or brown dots; dusky golden (bronze) with tarnished gold dots; unique to Ocicat are golden with cinnamon dots; chocolate with dull chocolate dots; sienna with beige or ecru dots; and lavender with lavender dots. Ground colors on which darker dots may appear range from pale silver through ivory, buff, and blue. Eyes are copper, green, yellow, hazel, or blue-green, and have dark lids rimmed with lightest color of coat. Nose leather and paw pads correspond to specific coat colors and range from pink to black.

Potential Health Problems
No known health problems. Basically hardy.

Care and Grooming
If proper diet is maintained, coat will be healthy and will require little grooming.

Kittens
Fairly large litters of 5 to 6 kittens. Kittens mature young, are large, outgoing, full of fun and vigor. They begin mother's diet at about 3 to 4 weeks, are allowed as much as they want until 8 months, and thereafter are fed twice daily. Both males and females are precocious; females comparatively dainty. Males must be altered by about 8 months. Great stamina.

Comment
The Ocicat originated in the United States in 1964 from second-generation breedings of Siamese and Abyssinians. The spotted tabby-patterned offspring were used to perpetuate the genetic inheritance, and they became the new Ocicat breed. The Ocicat was so named by its original breeder because of the first kitten's resemblance to a baby ocelot. Since then American Shorthairs have been introduced by some breeders for pattern and type, but the unique colors are probably the result of the Abyssinian influence. The breed was accepted for registration in the Cat Fanciers' Association in the 1960s, and a concerned group of breeders is presently working for advancement in that association.

Recommendations
Gentle, calm, and intelligent, the Ocicat is ideal for those who love the feral look without the feral temperament. A dramatically beautiful cat.

Plate 71

Oriental Shorthair

Characteristics
Siamese body type
Unusual coloring
with familiar patterns
Green eyes

Personality
Intelligent, witty, ebullient, graceful, and elegant. Devoted to people. Bright and charming companion. Adaptable, confident confidant. Nothing escapes this cat. Quite talkative.

Ideal Appearance
Medium-size. Breed standard almost identical to Siamese standard. The breeds differ only in 1 or 2 color genes. Oriental Shorthair is long, lithe, tubular, and leggy. Fine-boned. Long, tapering, wedge-shaped head. Large, flared ears carry out the wedge. Almond-shaped eyes. Long, whiplike tail. Short, fine, tight, hard coat.

Colors
Numerous colors unique to breed. Solid colors are blue, chestnut, cinnamon, cream, ebony, fawn, lavender, red, and white. Shaded colors include blue-cream silver, cameo, chestnut silver, chestnut-tortie silver, cinnamon silver, cinnamon-tortie silver, ebony silver, fawn silver, lavender-cream silver, lavender silver, and tortoiseshell silver. Smoke color class includes blue smoke, cameo smoke, chestnut smoke, cinnamon smoke, ebony smoke, fawn smoke, lavender smoke, and particolor smoke. Tabby colors include all solid colors as well as cameo, silver, blue silver, cinnamon silver, chestnut silver, and lavender silver in classic, mackerel, patched, spotted, and ticked tabby patterns. The particolor class includes blue-cream, cinnamon tortoiseshell, chestnut-tortie, fawn-cream, lavender-cream, and tortoiseshell. Orientals have green eyes. Whites may have blue or green eyes but not odd eyes. Nose leather and paw pads harmonize with coat color and range from pink to blue to black.

Potential Health Problems
Good health but prone to upper respiratory illnesses. Cardiomyopathy has occasionally occurred.

Care and Grooming
Little grooming required. Bathe only when necessary. High-protein, balanced feline diet needed to keep tensile, muscular body in top condition.

Kittens
Average of 5 pudgy kittens per litter. Kittens change drastically from day to day, but kitten born good usually gets better. Eye color not evident until 6 to 8 weeks, sometimes longer. Patterns and colors determined right away, except smokes and silvers. Some lines mature physically by 7 months; others take 2 years. Usually sexually precocious. Immaculately clean; some males spray, others do not. Females in season often spray.

Comment
The first CFA championship year for Oriental Shorthairs was the 1977–78 season. No other breed new to championship ever recorded as many top awards and grand champions as did the Oriental Shorthair that year. A hybrid, the Oriental Shorthair is a highly stylized, man-made cat. The idea originated in England in 1950, when breeders took the Siamese standard and applied new colors to the traditional body type. By 1968 a number of American breeders had Orientals, and by 1972 Orientals were registered in the Cat Fanciers' Association.

Recommendation
Like the Siamese, a breed for the connoisseur. The Oriental Shorthair is a chatty companion. It has definite preferences and prejudices. Not quite as impish as its Colorpoint Shorthair cousin, the Oriental Shorthair still has its silly moments. Extremely affectionate and dependent on people, it is totally empathetic to one special person.

Plates 65, 66, 67, 68

Russian Blue

Characteristics
Dense, plush,
beaverlike coat
Medium, wedge-
shaped head
Sinuous body
Blue with silver
tipping

Personality
Gentle, somewhat reserved. Extremely
soft-spoken, almost unintelligible. Very
affectionate toward mate and its owners,
but conservative with strangers. Can be
temperamental.

Ideal Appearance
Medium-size. Double plushy coat is
main physical characteristic. Short,
dense, fine coat like a beaver's. Feels soft
and silky. Head is smooth, with medium
wedge. Blunt muzzle, without
exaggerated pinch or whisker break.
Smooth top of head; flat line, angling
down from top of eyes to tip of nose.
Top of head longer than nose. Large ears
wide at base, tips more pointed than
rounded. Ear leather shows through,
with little hair either inside or outside.
Long, slender neck. Fine-boned, lithe,
graceful body, proportionate legs and
tail.

Colors
Bright, even blue, the outer or guard
hairs distinctly tipped, giving the cat a
silvery sheen. Definite contrast between
ground color and tipping. Vivid green
eyes. Nose leather is slate-gray; paw pads
are lavender-pink or mauve.

Potential Health Problems
No genetic problems. Healthy, alert,
and physically fit. Dense coat makes
Russian Blue hardy.

Care and Grooming
Coat should feel and look springy, alive,
and seem to stand up. Should not lie
perfectly flat. First brush backward
firmly, then gently stroke in proper
direction. Do not use grooming powder
except when showing. Bathe
occasionally. Feed balanced feline diet
with supplementary vitamins.

Kittens
Average litters of 4 kittens, which are
dependent on parents for several weeks.
Both parents rear kittens. Kittens grow
quickly, begin to eat around 5 weeks.
Coats thick and almost fuzzy until they
molt, then lose any faint shadow
barring. Prime age about 2 years.
Kittens are hardy, outgoing, and playful
within the family; easily frightened by
strangers.
Due to hybridization to Siamese during
World War II, Russian Blues may
produce "White Russians" in their
litters, which are blue-point Siamese in
coloration.

Comment
Russian Blues have been known by many
names. Because sailors allegedly brought
these cats from the White Sea port of
Archangel to Europe in the 1860s, they
were called Archangel; others dubbed
them Spanish Blue, Maltese Blue, and
even, for a brief period, British Blue.
During World War II, breeders were
forced to breed Russians to Siamese to
prevent their extinction (thus the so-
called White Russians that still occur
today). For a time, too, the type became
strikingly similar to Siamese, and not
until 1966 did a group of breeders
exclude the Siamese body type and
emphasize the intermediate build with
its typical plush coat. It took more than
20 years, as well as imports from Sweden
and Britain, to stabilize the type.
Recognized in American associations in
the late 1960s, the Russian Blue is
considered one of the oldest breeds.

Recommendation
This breed is so quiet you may not know
when a female is in season. It is a
conservative, reserved cat that enjoys
observing the activity around it.
Physically hardy and robust, the Russian
Blue is fine with children and dogs,
requires little discipline, and trains
easily. Males can be aggressive if
overhandled.

Plate 48

Scottish Fold

Characteristics
Folded ears, rounded skull
Well-padded, level body
Wistful expression
Prominent cheeks
Big, round eyes

Personality
Sweet-natured and friendly toward everyone. Its wistful expression seems to beg for cuddling. Gentle and placid. Innately courteous, respectful of people and property. Not very vocal.

Ideal Appearance
Medium-size. Known for its ears, which are folded forward and downward. Smaller, tighter fold preferred to larger, looser fold. Ears set in caplike fashion with rounded tips. Rounded head has prominent cheeks and whisker pads. Male tends to be jowly. Large, round eyes; sweet expression. Broad, short nose with gentle dip or brief stop but no break. Medium-size rounded body, amply padded. Level back. Firm stance on medium legs. Flexible tail. Short, dense, resilient coat.

Colors
There are 23 colors and patterns. Nose leather and paw pads coordinate with coat color, and eye color is same as American and British shorthairs. Colors include solid white, black, blue, red, and cream; shaded (tipped) colors of chinchilla, shaded silver, shell and shaded cameos, black, blue, and cameo smoke; classic or mackerel tabby in silver, red, brown, blue, cream, or cameo; patched tabby; and particolors in tortoiseshell, calico, dilute calico, blue-cream, and bicolor. Any other color acceptable except chocolate, lavender, and Himalayan pattern or these combined with white.

Potential Health Problems
Not a breed for the novice. Although generally hardy, ears are potential problem. Dominant gene that produces folded ears is nonlethal but can cause crippling when 2 folded-ear cats are bred together. Thickened, nonpliable limbs and/or tail indicate progressive fusion of spinal column. Tail may look blunted or like a bottlebrush. Lump on back leg, between knee and heel, may be calcium deposit, indicator of future trouble. Looser rather than tighter ear fold is better for pet. White cats may be deaf, requiring special care.

Care and Grooming
Ears need specific attention to prevent ear mites and infection. Once a week, gently clean interior with cotton swab dipped in solution of Merthiolate. Brush coat occasionally.

Kittens
Usually 5 kittens in litter, with only 2 kittens eventually developing folded ears. All born with straight ears, and ears start folding at 3 to 4 weeks. Ears can straighten from illness, tension, or nervous shock. Female's ears loosen when in season, male's when it is "calling."

Comment
The Scottish Fold is a natural mutation discovered on a Perthshire, Scotland, farm by a shepherd in 1961. Its development and recognition as a breed has become the subject of considerable controversy. The breed was first registered in England, but the privilege was later rescinded when it was found that the single dominant gene responsible for the folding ears could also cause severe crippling. American associations, however, did recognize the breed, and the cats have become popular —if rare—in this country. Scottish Folds were registered in the Cat Fanciers' Association in 1974 and received championship status in 1976.

Recommendation
The Scottish Fold is an excellent family cat, reserved but affectionate. It gets along well with other cats and with dogs. However, because of its special trait, the Scottish Fold needs extra care and is not for the careless owner.

Plates 41, 99, 100

Siamese

Characteristics
Long, lean, tubular body
Narrow, triangular head
Long, whiplike tail
High on legs
Vivid blue eyes

Personality
Extraordinarily intelligent, precocious, talkative, loyal, fearless, and willful. The Siamese thinks, plans, acts—sometimes tactlessly, always tactically. Moods swing from placid to prickly, arrogant to affectionate. Totally unpredictable.

Ideal Appearance
Medium-size. Svelte, sinuous, elegant, extremely refined, with long, tapering lines. Long, tapering, wedge-shaped head forms equilateral triangle from nose to tips of ears. Profile is absolutely straight from forehead to nose; no whisker pinch or nose dip. Eyes are almond-shaped, slanted toward nose in harmony with wedge. Fine, classic bones. Long, muscular, tubular body. Very tall on its legs. Long, tapered, whiplike tail. Coat is so short and tight as to be almost invisible.

Colors
Color is always restricted to points—mask, ears, tail, and feet. Point colors: seal, chocolate, blue, or lilac. Eye color always deep, vivid blue.

Potential Health Problems
Generally healthy. There has been some evidence of cardiomyopathy in Siamese, not related to any specific lines. Very susceptible to upper respiratory diseases prior to adulthood. Rarely ill once mature. May demonstrate a sensitivity to vaccines. Sensitive to anesthetics. Very rare cases of retinal dysplasia.

Care and Grooming
Short, tight coat needs little brushing. Cat takes care of its own grooming. This energetic breed needs room to play. Provide balanced, high-protein diet.

Kittens
Litters can be quite large, often 5 to 6 after a first litter of 4 kittens. Born white, kittens look like pink and white mice until color begins tinting ears and noses, then toes. Some lines are slow to develop and do not mature until at least 12 months. Kittens are incredibly intelligent, valiant, daring. Males spray less than other breeds, but females often spray when in season and are very vocal.

Comment
Although it is depicted in the ancient Siamese *Cat-Book Poems,* no one knows for certain when or where this distinctive pointed cat originated. Pictures dated A.D. 1350 from Ayutthaya, the old capital of Siam, show a much paler body color than the dark-bodied cats of central Russia depicted in 1793. But since the coat color of the Siamese is thermostatically controlled—the cooler the temperature, the darker the coat, accounting for the dense color at the extremities—the descriptions are probably of the same breed.
The earliest imports to Great Britain were described as 2 distinct colors—the pale-bodied, dark-pointed seal point, or Royal Siamese, and a chocolate-bodied, seal-pointed Chocolate Siamese; but the latter probably was the contemporary Tonkinese. English breeders concentrated on the Royal Siamese. The first Siamese breed standard was written in 1892; that cat looked very different from the svelte sophisticate we know now. The breed is, however, still not as extreme in Europe and Great Britain as it is in America.
The Cat Fanciers' Association in America recognizes only the 4 classic colors—chocolate, seal, lilac, and blue—as Siamese. In Great Britain and Europe, other colors are accepted.

Recommendation
The Siamese is a one-on-one cat. It will usually express devotion to one particular family member. It is a prima donna, inappropriate as a pet if you are an authoritarian but perfect if you want a very special friend.

Plates 43, 57, 58, 59, 60

Singapura

Characteristics
Ticked pattern
Huge, expressive eyes
Distinctly broad space
between eyes
Small size

Personality
Delightful, despite slight shyness.
Curiosity prevails. Playful and sociable.
An inquisitive charmer. Relatively quiet.

Ideal Appearance
Small with medium bone structure.
Characteristically ticked coat. Rounded
head, broad between eyes. Large eyes and
ears. Blunt nose on broad muzzle, with
slight stop below eye level. Definite
whisker pinch. Short, slightly thick
neck. Muscular body. Short, oval feet.
Medium-length tail. Coat is short, very
silky, tight on body. Extremely
beautiful, expressive eyes.

Colors
Same as Abyssinian pattern except that
barring on inner front leg and back knee
permitted. Warm, light tones preferred.
Brown ticking on yellow-tinged and
ivory ground. Chin, chest, and stomach
the color of unbleached muslin. Dark
brown lines around eyes, nose, lips,
whisker apertures, and between toes.
Salmon tones on ears and nose bridge
allowed. Nose leather pale to dark
salmon; paw pads rosy brown. Eyes are
hazel, green, or yellow.

Potential Health Problems
Generally healthy breed. Kittens may
react adversely to early vaccinations, but
they recover.

Care and Grooming
Requires diet high in potassium iodide;
otherwise, well-balanced feline nutrition
sufficient. No special grooming needs.

Kittens
Average of 4 kittens per litter. Kittens
develop color as Abyssinians do, with
ticking developing gradually. Lighter-
colored kittens will have better adult
color. Kittens very playful, comfortable
with their owners, wary with strangers
until better acquainted. Curiosity
overcomes shyness rapidly. Love
company of other cats. If allowed,
queens would nurse kittens until next
litter due.

Comment
The first Singapuras in the United States
were imported to California in 1975.
Successful breedings, despite initial
difficulties, have resulted in reasonable
availability for interested breeders and
pet owners. While this cat's coat color is
similar to that of the Abyssinian and the
pattern almost identical, the Singapura's
body type is quite different and its
wistful face unique. The breed, for
which one standard prevails, is accepted
for championship in all associations
except the Cat Fanciers' Association,
where it is registerable.

Recommendation
Said to be aggressively affectionate, the
Singapura is also known as a common-
sense cat because it rarely squabbles. It is
very sociable around people, even
visitors. Adults are as playful as kittens.
This cat involves itself intimately with
all facets of home life.

Plate 72

Snowshoe

Characteristics
Unique bicolor points
Modified wedge-
shaped head
Medium-size to large

Personality
Rather docile, quiet of voice. Vigorous, alert, intelligent. Enjoys the company of its owner; not a loner.

Ideal Appearance
Medium-size to large. Distinctive breed characteristic is bicolor points. Body type closer to American Shorthair than Siamese ancestry. Overall balance is important. Medium-boned, well-muscled, solid body with medium neck in proportion to body. Modified wedge head nearly an equilateral triangle, with high cheekbones. Nose rises slightly at bridge. Large, pointed ears are broad at base, set forward from outside of head. Large, oval eyes slant toward nose in harmony with lines of wedge. Medium-length, glossy, slightly coarse, close-lying coat. Medium-long, tapered tail.

Colors
Seal point or blue point. Light, even, subtly shaded body color. Points similar to those of Siamese, with white-tipped front paws, white chest, chin, and muzzle; hind legs white to the hock. Mask, tail, ears, and legs dense, clearly defined seal or blue, with masking covering entire face except for white-pattern areas; preferred pattern is inverted white V. May have eye mask. Nose may be white or point color or combination of both; paw pads pink, point color, or combination. Eyes are bright, sparkling blue.

Potential Health Problems
Generally healthy and vigorous. Breed is not well known yet.

Care and Grooming
Only routine grooming required. Cat should feel hard and muscular, and have heft but with no evidence of fat. A balanced feline diet will keep the cat in good condition.

Kittens
Litters average 4 to 5 kittens. Sturdy kittens develop physically like the American Shorthair, although color and pattern take several weeks to identify, like the Siamese. Kittens are affectionate and silly. Average weaning time.

Comment
The Snowshoe combines the heftiness of the American Shorthair and the litheness of the Siamese. Because of its ancestry, which includes American Shorthair bicolors, it is a unique combination of the Himalayan (point-restricted) pattern with a white spotting factor.

The breed's origins can be traced to the Kensing Cattery in Philadelphia, where 2 Siamese cats produced 3 females with white feet, the distinctive characteristic that led to the name Snowshoe. About 10 years later, in the mid-1970s, 2 breeders in the Midwest and another in Virginia worked with the breed, developed a standard, and achieved breed recognition in the Cat Fanciers' Federation. The CFF advanced the breed to championship status in 1983.

Recommendation
The greatest asset of this very attractive cat is its personality. Snowshoes are people-oriented and will follow their owners everywhere. They make excellent house pets.

Plate 91

Sphynx

Characteristics
Hairless
Body type a cross
between Devon Rex
and Cornish Rex
Skin feels oily
Very rare

Personality
Extremely affectionate, loving, sweet-natured. Purrs constantly. Very sensitive to mood, ambience, and environment.

Ideal Appearance
Tough, wrinkled, hairless skin is main characteristic of breed. Sweet facial expression, expressive eyes, huge ears. Body type a cross between that of Devon Rex and Cornish Rex. Long, camel-backed torso. Tall on legs. Long, whiplike tail.

Colors
All colors and patterns possible, but these look like tattoos because of hairlessness. Coat color distinguishable only when adorned with thin winter coat: on tufts behind ears, on nose, and at tip of tail. Eyes are usually gold but any color acceptable.

Potential Health Problems
Normal body temperature is 4 degrees higher than most other breeds. Unable to store fat, so requires frequent meals. Reproduction erratic. Queens may have difficulty rearing kittens, which may not be hardy. A lethal gene is suspected, but too few representatives of breed are available for in-depth genetic studies.

Care and Grooming
Because cat is utterly hairless except for thin down in winter, it must be protected from cold at all times. Should usually wear a sweater. When in coat, down on body very fragile and easily damaged. However, skin exudes oil, requiring regular bathing with detergent-type shampoo. High metabolism requires that cats be fed frequently, but they can eat all they want without gaining weight.

Kittens
Sphynx to Sphynx breedings have produced no known viable litters. Most known examples of the breed have been spontaneous mutations, or anomalies, in unexpected domestic or Rex litters. According to one source, Sphynx bred to coated shorthairs produce hairless, wiry-haired, and curly-haired kittens, with little likelihood of hairless kittens.

Comment
Much myth surrounds this hairless breed of cat, which may or may not have a South American origin. The breed is not related to the Chihuahua dog, despite its similar skin texture and some doglike mannerisms.

The Sphynx was first introduced to cat fanciers via breeding programs and a resulting standard developed at a cattery in Ontario, Canada. The breed was proposed to the Cat Fanciers' Association for recognition, but the cats were not accepted. Most known examples have been found as strays or adopted "accidents." Although occasionally a Sphynx is seen on exhibition at cat shows in the United States, the pedigree is not widely recognized among associations, and very few of these cats are bred.

Recommendation
The Sphynx is very dependent on people for survival. It adores body contact with its owner or other pets and is affectionate and intelligent. This cat is not for everyone; it is a special breed for a special owner.

Plate 106

Tonkinese

Characteristics
Medium-size
Modified wedge-
shaped head
Distinctive color-
coordinated pattern
Aqua eyes
Minklike coat

Personality
Clever, active, witty, intelligent, fearless, and willful. Tends to be mischievous. Combines the best of Siamese and Burmese. Does well as a pair. Gets along with children and dogs. Loyal and loving.

Ideal Appearance
Medium-size. Moderate in every physical aspect. Muscular, solid build, surprisingly heavy for its size. Females average 5 to 6 pounds; males can be much larger, 9 to 12 pounds. Head is modified wedge, with slight dip between eyes and pinch at whisker. Ears pricked slightly forward. Eyes are open almond-shaped, slanted along sculptured cheekbones. Medium-length torso, tail, and legs. Oval paws. Short, glossy, close-lying coat feels like mink.

Colors
Siamese-patterned cats in 5 unique breed colors, with densely colored mask, ears, feet, and tail. But unlike Siamese, coat color is dilution of point color, shading gradually lighter on underparts. Natural mink, blue mink, champagne mink, platinum mink, and honey mink. Naturals have brown nose leather and paw pads; blues have blue nose leather and paw pads; champagnes, cinnamon nose leather and paw pads; platinums, pink; and honeys, pink to cinnamon. All have characteristic aqua eyes.

Potential Health Problems
Usually hardy. Low resistance to upper respiratory disease as kittens, like other Oriental breeds. May be sensitive to particular vaccines, and gas anesthetics are preferred to intravenous procedures.

Care and Grooming
Groom by stripping coat with a rubber brush to remove dead hair; follow with a chamois shine. Occasional bathing helps keep coat lively. Cat trees are imperative for these height-loving, indoor, aerial artists. Tonkinese do well on a meat-heavy, balanced feline diet plus vitamins.

Kittens
Rarely fewer than 3 kittens to a litter, most litters much larger. Queens deliver easily, and nurse for months, if allowed. Lighter colored at birth, only natural mink and solid sable kittens identifiable. Mother's diet must be supplemented, as babies are extremely demanding. Kittens rarely ready for new homes before 12 to 16 weeks. Males usually spray. Females may begin calling at about 8 months.

Comment
Tonkinese are a hybrid cross between Siamese and Burmese. The first known Tonkinese, though not so named, is thought to be Wong Mau, ancestress of the Burmese. However, documents indicate that the chocolate Siamese shown in England in the late 1800s were also Siamese-Burmese hybrids. From the 1950s through the early 1970s, scattered breeders worked with the Tonkinese in the United States and Canada.
The Tonkinese was first registered as a breed by the Canadian Cat Association in 1974, but it was not until 1978 that the Cat Fanciers' Association accepted the Tonkinese, and in 1984 the breed received championship status.
Today Tonkinese can be bred only to Tonkinese. It is the only breed that can consistently utilize its variant kittens to reproduce the breed.

Recommendation
Known for its shenanigans, the Tonkinese is an acrobat. It is practically a constant showstopper, demanding an attentive owner. It is thoroughly sociable, gregarious, and vocal. However, this innate prankster should not be trusted around bird cages. A cat with personality.

Plates 55, 56

Health Care

Before You Purchase a Cat

Cats are basically healthy animals if given proper care from the time they are born. Nevertheless, when you purchase a cat, you want to be sure that there are not any health problems. Because some illnesses may not be immediately apparent, the bill of sale from a reputable breeder, cattery, or pet shop should include an option to return the cat within fourteen days. A full refund or replacement should be guaranteed if a veterinarian certifies that the animal has a valid health problem. This two-week period covers the incubation time for most common infectious diseases. Any illness developing after two weeks should not be blamed on the breeder, since it probably was contracted after purchase. Certain breeds may be prone to inherited health problems. Maladies such as congenital heart defects or deafness may not be evident until weeks or months after a cat is purchased. Some breeders will replace kittens that show signs of inherited health problems, but these arrangements are usually voluntary, and the breeders involved are truly interested in the improvement of their breed. Of course, after several weeks of ownership, most people have fallen in love with their pet and do not want to trade it. The seller may therefore insist, by prior agreement, that affected cats be neutered so they cannot reproduce and pass on undesirable traits.

Before purchasing a cat, it is wise to read as much as you can about the breed you are considering. Check the Potential Health Problems section in each breed account and, at the end of this chapter, refer to the list rating the seriousness of health problems. It is important to ask a breeder about the history of a cat's parents. Talk with breeders, other owners, or local veterinarians to see if there are any serious problems associated with this breed.

At the time of purchase, ask the seller what you should do if your kitten develops some inherited problem. Certain congenital abnormalities such as extra toes, a bent tail, or unusual coat or eye color may disqualify the cat from breeding and show, but they do not affect its health or detract from the animal's suitability as a pet. To prevent future health difficulties, it is essential to take your cat for a complete veterinary examination within a few days of purchase.

Living Quarters

Once you have taken your kitten home, you must decide where it will sleep. A household pet needs only a padded box or basket to call its own—a comfortable refuge for rest and seclusion. Put the box in an out-of-the-way corner of a room or a part of the house that is acceptable to you.

A cat kept outdoors—a healthier situation—requires a tight, dry house to protect it from wind and weather. The house should be big enough for your pet to stand up and turn around in easily, but not so large that its body heat will not keep it warm. Loose bedding and a cloth flap over the door can help keep your cat snug in cold weather. The house should be built for easy cleaning and treating with insecticides to control parasites. A box about the size of a big mailbox is ideal for most cats. Even if your pet spends most of its time indoors, an alternate outdoor home is great as an emergency shelter during storms and suits the cat's territorial social habits. Fresh, clean water should always be available nearby.

Choosing the Right Cat Food

Selecting a cat food can be extremely confusing, since there are so many types and brands available. Contrary to some advertising promotion, cats do not need flavor variety in their food. However, they may become addicted to one particular food, so it is best to vary the menu occasionally. Nutrition should be carefully balanced.

Although cats are classified as carnivores, they do not do well on an exclusive diet of meat. Their wild ancestors ate a balanced diet by consuming the entire carcasses of the game they caught—meat, bone, hair, and the vegetable matter their prey had eaten earlier—but modern cats cannot.

Today cats still require a balanced diet, and the best cat foods provide many different ingredients, carefully compounded to provide all the required amino acids (protein), fats, and carbohydrates, as well as essential vitamins and minerals. Commercial foods are far superior to diets composed of ingredients found in our own kitchens. Leftover table food can be used to feed cats but is not satisfactory. Cats should not be fed dog food, which is too low in protein and fat for feline needs. Most of the cat's meal should be a proven, balanced and complete commercial cat food.

Cat foods are sold either as complete and balanced diets or as special gourmet foods that are not complete. Always use the balanced diet as the basic food. If treats or snacks are also given, a single day's supply of the treat should be calculated as part of the cat's daily food consumption. The best way to control the quantity of snacks is to place a day's supply in a covered dish out of the cat's reach. Reward your cat with these tidbits until the dish is empty, and do not offer any more for the rest of the day. If you follow a consistent feeding plan, your cat will not be overfed and it will not become fat.

The basic types of commercial cat foods each have special characteristics. Some cats like dry and crunchy food; others prefer it sloppy and moist. Some owners want their cats to feed themselves; others seek an inexpensive, easy-to-store product; and still others like to pamper their pet with different foods. One type of commercial cat food will probably meet your needs and those of your cat. However, if your cat has particular problems with its diet and is very thin or very fat, or has frequent digestive upsets, you should seek veterinary advice.

Dry Cat Foods
These foods contain eight to ten percent water and are a mixture of cereals, meat by-products, and vegetable protein (soy) combined with vegetable and animal fats, vitamins, and minerals. The ingredients are compressed into small, irregular, crunchy cubes or puffs that are sprayed with fat, forming products known as expanded foods. Their high content of animal protein, animal fat, and moisture improve the palatability or flavor. Because cats taste the fat on the outside, they like it better; they also feel full sooner because the food is bulky. It has fewer calories per ounce than denser foods, so there is less tendency to overeat. Cats are nibblers and most prefer food that is dry and crunchy. And many owners prefer the expanded food, since a big bag is relatively lightweight for the volume it contains and is economical as well.

Expanded dry foods are very suitable as a base diet for self-feeding schedules, in which a cat essentially feeds itself when hungry. To accustom a cat to self-feeding, place a large pan of food before the cat just after it has been satiated by a regular feeding. Eventually the cat will nibble at its new food and then eat a small amount fifteen or twenty times a day. You must never let the food dish become empty. Since there are no leftovers, this method does not waste food, and the cat will not beg at feeding time, because there is none: Food is available at all times. Although a few self-fed cats overeat and become obese, most adjust their food intake to balance their energy needs for exercise, keeping warm, and maintaining their ideal body weight.

Semi-moist Foods

These foods contain 25 to 30 percent water and are usually packaged in cellophane or plastic pouches in the form of small pellets or bits in various shapes. They are all balanced, high-protein foods and, although they look like meat, are composed mostly of meat by-products, textured soybean meal, cereals, and chemical agents added to prevent spoilage and keep the product moist. Semi-moist foods no longer have the high levels of salt or sugar that were used to prevent spoilage in the first products. Because semi-moist foods are rich in calories and protein and are highly palatable and easily digested, they are good for tempting fussy eaters. Broken up and moistened with milk or water to make a gruel, they are also useful for feeding young kittens or ill animals. They cannot be used for self-feeding, however; normal cats may overeat when fed these foods unless you watch the amount carefully. Once the plastic seal of the packaging is broken, some of these products dry out rapidly, become less palatable, and spoil.

Canned (Moist) Foods

This type of food contains 70 to 80 percent water and is highly palatable, but also expensive, although cats consume so little that cost is usually insignificant. Canned foods cannot be used for self-feeding and do not promote good tooth and gum condition. Many canned foods are classified as gourmet foods and contain ingredients such as chicken, liver, kidney, or shrimp, with special sauces or flavorings. Some are not balanced, complete foods. These products cater to the owner rather than the cat and are not recommended, especially as a staple. They may look as if they are composed entirely of muscle meat, but in reality they contain a

variety of animal by-products with textured vegetable protein dyed red to look like meat. Always check the label for contents.

If a product is balanced and complete, the label will say so. In contrast to the so-called gourmet foods, complete canned foods resemble meat pudding and contain animal by-products (with cereals or soy meal as binders) as well as vitamins and minerals to meet cats' nutritional requirements. Because of their excellent palatability, they are good for fussy eaters. However, if you are not careful, normal animals may become obese by overeating. One advantage of canned foods is that the small size of the containers makes them convenient to serve as individual meals. Store any leftovers in the refrigerator, but be certain to warm the food to room temperature before serving it to your pet to avoid causing digestive upset.

Homemade Diets and Dietary Supplements

Food prepared at home is rarely balanced and adequate for a cat. Homemade dishes should not be used routinely for long periods unless they are carefully formulated by a nutritionist. Even then, most people do not have the discipline to prepare special items every day. The best advice here is not to use a homemade diet.

Healthy cats rarely need dietary supplements. Rather than helping your pet, these foods may upset the ratio of nutrients in carefully balanced commercial diets. Extra does not mean better. Too much supplementation may cause serious problems in growing kittens. Vitamin and mineral powders, vitamin tablets, natural food products, and other supplements are usually a waste of money. Use them only if directed by your veterinarian.

Special Diets

At certain times in its life, a cat may

require a special diet. Some foods are designed especially for growth, pregnancy and lactation, or weight loss. Others are intended to treat special diseases that must be managed in part by modifying or regulating food intake. Growth or weight-loss foods are designed to fulfill special physiological needs; they can be purchased from a grocery store or your veterinarian. Disease-treatment products are available only from veterinarians. They serve as part of a medical treatment and, although expensive, are worth the cost. Some are used for only a few weeks; others may be needed for the pet's lifetime. A recently introduced diet has been extremely effective in reducing one type of urinary problem common in male cats.

Feeding Schedule

How often and how much should you feed your cat? When you bring your new cat home—whether kitten or adult—do not try to change its diet drastically. Feed the cat the same food on the same schedule it was on before. Later you may want or need to change this program, but do it gradually over a period of several days.

Soon after you bring your new cat home, weigh it. You will want to watch the weight gain in a kitten or to make sure the weight of a full-grown cat is constant. Your veterinarian can give you a growth chart showing the ideal weight for your cat at different stages of its life. Then you should feed your cat amounts that allow it to maintain a weight corresponding to its weight on the growth curve.

Kittens and pregnant or lactating queens need high-protein, high-calorie concentrated food. They should be fed two or three times daily. For each feeding provide only what they can consume in about ten minutes. Kittens require about twice the amount of food needed by adult cats. The amount to

feed is usually specified on the package. Watch your kitten's progress and feed it accordingly. Kittens should grow well but be slightly thin, active, tough, and muscular, with shiny coats. It is not desirable to push them for rapid growth and get them roly-poly fat. Do not overfeed. Exercise, environmental temperature, a cat's metabolic rate, special physiological needs, and temperament all combine to determine food requirements.

After your kitten matures, in about twelve months, keep its weight constant. Weigh the kitten monthly and increase or decrease the food as needed.

Feed an adult cat once daily—in the evening if you want it active during the day, and in the morning if you want an alert cat at night. Cats, like people, get sleepy after eating. Cats like to nibble, so self-feeding, or having dry food available at all times, is a good way to feed. It is important to establish a sound feeding routine early and develop good habits.

Exercise

Cats usually determine exercise levels for themselves. Staying fit may help a cat live its nine lives successfully. Outdoor cats get much more exercise than indoor pets, since their social habits keep them patrolling and defending their territories constantly. To stimulate indoor cats to be more playful, provide scratching posts, catnip, and other toys suspended from a string. If you are able to keep two cats, they will practically exercise themselves—wrestling and playing together and thus receiving both physical and emotional stimulation.

Choosing a Veterinarian

When you take your new kitten to your veterinarian for its first physical examination, you will be told about vaccinations, parasites, feeding, behavior problems, and many other subjects that will enable you to understand the needs

of your cat. Be sure to have this initial
evaluation. It is important to establish a
rapport with a veterinarian who can be
an available, trusted advisor.
Before choosing a veterinarian, make
sure that the office, clinic, or hospital is
clean and well equipped. It should be
conveniently located and open at hours
that are reasonable for you. It should be
covered by a twenty-four-hour emergency
service. This is most important. The staff
should be friendly and enjoy caring for
your pet. The veterinarian's personality
should mesh with yours, and the charges
should be acceptable to you. You and the
veterinarian will act as a team to provide
the health care your cat will need over
the course of many years.

Vaccinations
The mystique of knowing which shot to
have administered at what time is
needlessly confusing. Kittens usually
have natural protection against disease
until they are weaned, and only then do
they require vaccinations. At your first
visit to the veterinarian, you will
probably receive a vaccination schedule.
To help you know what to expect,
consult the schedule of required
vaccinations on page 133.
When a kitten is born, it is vital that it
nurse on its mother during the first
twenty-four hours to get the colostrum,
or first milk. This milk contains special
proteins and antibodies that can protect
it against infectious diseases to which its
mother is immune. The kitten can
absorb these antibodies only during its
first day. If the queen has been
vaccinated against many diseases, the
kitten will also be protected, after
ingesting the first milk, for as long as
fourteen to sixteen weeks. If the mother
has a low level of resistance to a disease
—or no resistance at all—the kitten will
not be protected, or its protection will
wane quickly in several weeks.
Once the protection from the mother has

All cats require annual revaccination for these diseases; for rabies, some states require revaccination only every 3 years. The exact schedule may vary depending on the type of vaccines used and the exposure potential for individual cats.

*Vaccination may not be indicated for all cats. See your veterinarian for specific recommendations.

Vaccination Schedule	First	Second	Third
8 weeks			
Pneumonitis	●		
8–10 weeks			
Calicivirus	●		
Feline Leukemia Virus*	●		
Panleucopenia	●		
Rhinotracheitis	●		
12–14 weeks			
Calicivirus		●	
Feline Leukemia Virus*		●	
Panleucopenia		●	
Rhinotracheitis		●	
12–16 weeks			
Rabies	●		
2–4 months			
Feline Leukemia Virus*			●

waned, vaccinations must be given before the kitten becomes exposed to diseases. To reduce the risks of infectious diseases as much as possible, start vaccinations when your kitten is about six weeks old, repeat every two weeks until sixteen weeks old, and then give yearly booster shots. However, if you obtain a kitten that is about seven to eight weeks old (an ideal time for the kitten to be separated from its mother), vaccinations at eight, twelve, and sixteen weeks are usually adequate. A kitten purchased from a reputable dealer probably will have received some vaccinations already, depending on its age. If you have an older kitten, fewer injections will be needed.

It is crucial that at sixteen weeks or slightly later your kitten receive one vaccination for each major disease. These vaccinations are generally combined in two or three injections. Until your kitten has had a fairly complete vaccination series, keep the cat relatively isolated so that it is not exposed to infection. Vaccinations are a great health bargain: Do not skimp on them or fail to keep them current. They are often packaged in combinations that help minimize both the cost and the number of injections necessary. It is particularly important that your cat receive booster vaccinations before boarding, attending cat shows, or beginning pregnancy.

Rabies

For public health reasons—animal and human health—it is the law in most areas to keep pets currently vaccinated against rabies. In many parts of the United States and Canada, rabies has become increasingly common in wildlife, especially foxes, skunks, raccoons, and bats. Incidence of rabies in cats is becoming more frequent, especially in parts of the Midwest, where skunk rabies is common; because cats often associate with these animals, in such areas they are

at greater risk of exposure to the disease. Rabid animals act "funny": They may be especially affectionate or tame, when they should be wild and furtive. Pets can be bitten by a rabid animal without their owners' knowing it. After several weeks or sometimes months of incubation, the bitten animal can develop rabies. Rabies is fatal to people and other warm-blooded animals. Therefore it is imperative that you do your part to control this disease by keeping your pet's rabies vaccination current. Many communities provide free rabies vaccination clinics. One type of rabies vaccine for cats requires a booster only every third year; the other type available must be administered annually. The injection must be given in the muscle of a rear leg and can occasionally produce temporary lameness, but that is a small matter. Rabies vaccines offer excellent protection from a devastating disease.

Cat Distemper (Panleucopenia)

This viral disease is a great killer of kittens and unvaccinated cats. It produces symptoms of vomiting, diarrhea, fever, and depression, and depresses the production of white blood cells. Affected cats may die in just a few days, so prompt treatment is needed. Some cats may have very mild signs and recover easily; they then have lifelong immunity. Vaccines give rapid, effective protection for at least one year and must never be overlooked or postponed. Annual revaccination is recommended, especially if your pet will be exposed to other cats.

Feline Respiratory Disease

Respiratory disease in cats— rhinotracheitis, calicivirus, and pneumonitis—may be caused by either of two viral agents and/or a bacteria-like organism. Often more than one organism is involved, so it is essential to vaccinate for all three.

Rhinotracheitis

A highly contagious upper respiratory disease, rhinotracheitis is often fatal in kittens, but causes only a bad cold in most adult cats. Recovery gives protection against the severe systemic disease. However, when cats that have recovered from rhinotracheitis are under stress, they may have frequent, minor coldlike symptoms. Recovered cats that appear well themselves may shed the virus intermittently—in watery secretions from the eyes and nose, and especially in saliva—and thus may infect other cats. Two types of vaccine are available, one given by injection, the other by drops placed in the eyes and nose. Cats vaccinated by the drops may develop a mild cold about a week later. Both types of vaccine give reasonably good protection for about one year.

Calicivirus

This infection also produces cold symptoms in cats. It may also cause raw ulcers on the lips and tongue. Although recovery offers immunity, the virus is spread constantly to susceptible cats through the recovered animal's saliva. The vaccine for this disease is similar to that for rhinotracheitis, and in fact the two vaccines are usually combined and given simultaneously as an injection or as drops placed in the nose. Yearly revaccination is necessary for optimum protection.

Pneumonitis

Caused by a bacteria-like agent, pneumonitis produces a chronic respiratory infection involving the lungs more than the nose and eyes. This infection is less common than rhinotracheitis and calicivirus, but is still troublesome. Vaccination by a single injection provides protection for one year.

Feline Infectious Peritonitis

This widespread, complex viral disease is usually fatal to cats. It occurs in several forms, and in early stages may mimic other diseases. Blood tests are helpful but not always conclusive in diagnosis. Clinical signs of the disease in its most common form are depression, poor appetite, weight loss, and enlargement of the abdomen due to accumulated fluid. The immediate future offers no cure: Attempts to develop a vaccine for this insidious disease so far have not been fruitful.

Nonetheless, there are precautions you can take to protect your pet against infection. One way to control infection in groups of cats is to administer blood tests to identify which cats may be infected. These animals should then be isolated to prevent further spread of the disease. If you already have healthy cats at home and acquire a new cat, make sure that it has been tested negative for feline infectious peritonitis within thirty days of the date it joins your household. As a routine precaution, you can easily kill the virus in litter boxes and food dishes by disinfecting with a dilution of one part household chlorine bleach in thirty parts water.

Feline Leukemia Virus

The most important fatal infectious disease of domestic cats today, feline leukemia is caused by a virus that is spread in all secretions of an infected cat, especially in the saliva. Cats contract the disease by ingesting the virus, which is easily transmitted via grooming, sneezing, fighting, and other feline social contact, as well as by sharing food dishes and litter boxes.

Kittens under six months of age are especially susceptible, while older cats tend to resist infection, at least initially. Some cats may sustain a subclinical infection (showing no visible signs of illness) that handicaps their immune system, lowering their resistance to stress and to other diseases. Affected cats are abnormally susceptible to bacterial, fungal, and viral infections. In this condition even the stress of minor surgery, a small accident, coming into season, boarding, or the owner's absence may predispose infected cats to diseases a normal cat would repel easily.

Feline leukemia virus may also cause blood or lymph node cancer in cats, resulting in a short life expectancy for most that test positive for this disease. Cats testing positive for the virus should be removed from a multiple-cat household to protect the normal cats. The words cancer and contagion are unsettling to everyone. But epidemiological studies have offered no conclusive evidence that humans are at any increased risk of developing leukemia or other tumors as a result of exposure to leukemia-positive cats.

A vaccine is now available to protect cats from feline leukemia. Vaccination should be preceded by a blood test. If the test is negative, the cat should receive an initial series of three vaccinations—the first shot is followed by a second one three weeks later, and the second is followed by a third two to four months later—and then an annual booster. The vaccine is thought to be about 80 percent effective, but is of no value to cats already exposed to or infected by the disease. A few cats may have local pain from the intramuscular injection.

Intestinal Parasites

Cats have more fastidious toilet habits than dogs and thus have fewer problems with worms, or intestinal parasites. They can, however, mean serious trouble for young kittens and may pose a threat to kittens and adult cats alike in warm, humid climates. Some worms can be transmitted to people. Yet many cat owners are unduly concerned about worms and overworm their pets. In most environments, these intestinal parasites are rarely a problem at all.

Signs of Worms and Effective Control

Diarrhea and/or unthriftiness are the most common signs of the presence of worms. If you suspect that your kitten has worms, it is best to consult your veterinarian. The veterinarian will probably want to examine a stool sample microscopically to make an accurate diagnosis and prescribe the correct drug. Some medications are effective only for certain parasites. If you use the wrong medication, there is no benefit. Moreover, worm remedies are poisonous and should not be given if unwarranted. If your cat is ill from something other than worms or in addition to these parasites, needless or even normal worming may be harmful.

The control of worms involves much more than administering drugs. Obviously the best control is to prevent your cat from becoming infected. But sometimes this is impossible. For example, a kitten can become infected while nursing or even while still in its mother's uterus.

If a cat has worms, treatment requires breaking the parasite's life cycle. By definition, a parasite is an organism that lives on or in a host animal, which provides many or all of the parasite's needs. If those needs can be removed or reduced, or if the parasite can be attacked at some stage of its life when it is outside the host, control can be safer and more effective than when only worm medications are used.

There are three major kinds of intestinal parasites that affect cats: Roundworms and hookworms most commonly affect young kittens; tapeworms can pose problems to cats of all ages.

Roundworms

Ascarids, or roundworms, can cause severe illness and even death in kittens. Sometimes they infect kittens before birth, but they can also be ingested after birth. As a cat matures, it gradually develops a tolerance to roundworms, and can even live comfortably with a few parasites still inside its intestines. Roundworms lay eggs, which pass to the outside in the stool. When the eggs are eaten by another or the same cat, the infestation spreads. The eggs hatch and immature worms, or larvae, wander through the new host's body tissues. They eventually return to the intestines, where they develop into mature egg-producing worms; then the cycle is repeated.

Worms migrating inside the body cannot be contacted and killed by drugs administered orally. This, together with repeated ingestion of eggs from the queen's milk or the kittens' stools, is the reason that repeated doses of medications are needed. Better control will be possible when new drugs are developed that eliminate the parasites from all tissues in the body.

Certain types of roundworms are a matter of public health concern because they may spread from cats and dogs to children. The larvae migrate into the children's tissues just as they do in the pets' bodies. Children can ingest the eggs, too. Parasite eggs can be consumed by children who eat sand or dirt from an animal's toilet area (the most frequent means of infection). Children's sandboxes should be covered when not in use to keep pets out. Children should not kiss pets or share food with them. With common sense sanitation, these concerns should be minimal.

Hookworms

Especially serious to kittens, hookworms suck blood from the wall of the intestine. Cats affected with large numbers of these parasites can die of anemia from severe blood loss. Hookworms are contracted through the queen's milk or by ingestion of the parasite's eggs, or they may penetrate the skin to enter a pet's body.

Control requires periodic worming, cleaning, and treatment of infected soil to kill eggs and parasite larvae. Dirt, grass runs, or shady pens often harbor the stages of the worm that live outside the cat. Cat hookworms are almost never a menace to people. They can be troublesome in catteries or places where groups of cats congregate or are housed together, because it is difficult to clean the premises effectively to prevent reinfection. These parasites are, however, much less common in cats than in dogs. Individual pets can almost always be successfully treated and permanently freed of hookworms.

Tapeworms

Easily treated with medications, these parasites rarely cause severe damage. The head of a tapeworm attaches itself to the lining of the cat's intestine. Small segments of the worm containing eggs break off periodically and appear in the stool as small, flattened objects that look like rice. To get rid of tapeworms, the heads must be removed by medication, and the tapeworm eggs must not be allowed to hatch. These eggs can develop only if they have a second host other than the cat, such as fleas, mice, rabbits, or regular food animals. When the cat consumes the raw viscera of the second host, the life cycle is completed. If you prevent your cat from eating the second host, tapeworms can be eliminated. Cooking food the cat eats effectively destroys all parasites. Direct ingestion of tapeworm segments by a cat will not cause infection.

One-celled Parasites

Toxoplasmosis is caused by a one-celled parasite that lives in the cat's intestine. Its eggs are shed in the cat's feces, and many birds and virtually all mammals, including humans, can become infected by ingesting the matured eggs from material contaminated with cat stool. (It takes several days for the eggs in the

Pilling a Cat
Wrap the cat in a towel. Open the mouth and insert tablet. Using the eraser end of a pencil, tap the back of the throat to stimulate the swallowing reflex. Quickly withdraw pencil and tap cat's nose. When the cat licks its nose, it swallows the pill.

stool to become infective.) The parasites then spread into the tissues of the intermediate host. The intermediate host animal may develop the clinical disease, or may develop immunity and never become ill. The disease is often contracted when one animal eats the raw flesh of an intermediate host. For this reason people who like undercooked or rare meat are at some risk. Pregnant women are further advised to avoid contact with infected cats or with cat litter boxes to prevent possible infection of the baby.

You can help prevent toxoplasmosis by following these steps. Clean the cat's litter box *daily;* Mature eggs in the stool become infective after a few days. Wash your hands thoroughly after handling the cat or the litter. Do not allow the cat to eat from your plate. Ensure that the cat eats only cooked food (commerical diets are fine). Unfortunately, it is nearly impossible to prevent a cat that is allowed outdoors from eating mice, birds, or other wildlife that are prime sources of toxoplasma infection. But by taking these precautions you can reduce the chances for the disease to spread. If your cat's blood tests positive for toxoplasmosis, discuss the test results and a management program with your veterinarian. If you or other members of your family become infected, seek the advice of your physician.

How to Prevent and Control Worms
Prevention and control of intestinal parasites can be complex; multiple infections are common, so specific diagnosis by a veterinarian is essential. Usually this is best done by microscopic examination of a stool specimen. Many treatment measures can and should be taken at home. Most medications are pills or liquids given orally but a few can be added to your pet's food. The diagrams at the top of these pages will show you how to give your pet pills.

Steps to Control Parasitic Infection
1. Obtain a specific diagnosis and proper directions for treatment.
2. Use good sanitary practices:
a. Pick up and dispose of stool daily.
b. Never feed your pet on the ground. Use a clean dish.
c. Use parasite-inhibiting agents on the ground if pets are confined to small pens.
3. Control intermediate hosts to break the parasite's life cycle:
a. Keep your cat from eating raw food, such as mice, rabbits, or birds.
b. Control fleas and other insects with insecticides or regular spray programs.
4. Administer the correct drug at the proper intervals for as long as necessary to eliminate the worms.
5. Apply all of these measures. Used alone, no one control is entirely satisfactory.

Fleas and Other External Parasites
Cats are susceptible to many external parasites that live on or are embedded in the surface of the skin. Fleas, lice, ticks, and mange mites are perhaps the most common pests. Most are easy to control with systematic treatment.

Fleas
The most difficult external parasites to control and probably the most common, fleas affect most cats at some time in their lives. Fleas are especially troublesome where the climate is humid and temperate all year, such as in the southeastern United States and along the California coast. At high altitudes, in dry climates, and in areas where there is a long winter season, these parasites are more easily controlled.

Fleas are small, brown, rapidly moving jumping insects that spend a large part of their lives off the host. The cat flea is the most common on both cats and dogs. They will bite many host animals—cats, dogs, rodents, and even people—if cats or dogs are not available. Fleas can live for over a year, and their eggs, found in

Pilling a Cat
Another way to pill a cat is to open the mouth with one hand and use forceps or tweezers to drop the tablet deep into the animal's throat. Withdraw the forceps quickly and tap cat's nose. When it licks its nose, the job is done.

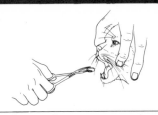

cracks in the floor, in cool basements, or in sandy areas, may last even longer. Fleas often bite around the base of a pet's tail, but they may attack other areas of the body, too. The bite may cause an initial local reaction, but as your pet becomes sensitized to flea bites, a more generalized reaction may occur, causing a rash to appear on many parts of the skin. This reaction is called flea allergy dermatitis and is the bane of many sensitive cats.

Controlling fleas requires a double-barreled attack: eliminating the fleas from your pet and your premises. Killing fleas on your cat demands persistence. Powders, sprays, and collars—in order of decreasing effectiveness—must be used thoroughly and regularly. Flea collars are less effective than other control measures. In trying to control fleas, all animals in the household, not just cats, must be treated.

Eliminating fleas from your home, a cat's bed, favorite chair, and other places the cat commonly frequents is usually relatively easy and can be done with a commercial product. Only the most severe infestations require a professional exterminator. Many new long-acting insecticides can be obtained at farm and garden stores. One new type of product prevents immature fleas from developing, and another provides safe, long-term killing action against fleas that invade the living area. The combination is highly successful.

Cats with flea allergies present a special dilemma. Some pets need veterinary care and additional treatment with cortisonelike drugs in order to get relief. Although cats may be affected by other skin allergies caused by food or inhaled pollens, fleas are by far the most common cause of allergic skin disease.

Lice
These tiny parasites cause intense itching, but are easily controlled with flea powders or sprays repeated weekly for three or four applications. Look for dandruff-like eggs attached to the hair shafts and adult lice on the surface of the skin.

Ticks
Common in woods, fields, and along sandy beaches, ticks attach themselves to the skin, especially around the ears and toes. Ticks can be removed with powders or can be picked off individually. Never use the tip of a hot cigarette to burn the tick.

The easiest way to remove this pest is to dab the tick with a generous quantity of alcohol for several minutes to stupefy it, and then pull it off gently with tweezers. Place the tick in a jar of alcohol to kill it. Most ticks attach themselves firmly by embedding their mouthparts in the cat's skin. If these pests are picked off with force, the mouthparts may remain embedded. Although this is not a major concern, it can be avoided by allowing time for the alcohol to act so that you can gently remove the entire tick.

Mange Mites
Several different types of mites can afflict cats. Some live in the ears or on the surface of the skin (otodectic mange and cheyletiella mange); others burrow into the skin (notoedric mange). Surface mites and notoedric manges are contagious and cause intense itching. They are quite easily cured by insecticides. Usually each case needs to be treated several times, and because of the contagion, all animals in contact must also be treated. Some of these animal manges cause temporary skin problems in people, but these are contracted only by very intimate contact and are easily cured.

Ear Mites
Especially common in kittens are ear mites, which produce a black granular discharge in the ear canal. Cleaning the

ears daily with mineral oil and dusting the kitten with flea powder usually solves the problem.

Grubs

Cutevebra larvae, or grubs, are wormlike parasites that may affect kittens during the late summer. Evidence of this pest is a lump with a slight hole in the center, usually in the skin around the kitten's neck or chest. The moving grub is about three-fourths of an inch long and may be seen at the entrance to the hole. Treatment requires anesthesia and veterinary care.

Pros and Cons of Neutering

Some pet owners are troubled by discussion of neutering cats so that they cannot breed. Neutering means removing the reproductive glands, which does not affect the cat's health. Spaying the female involves removal of the ovaries and uterus; castrating the male removes the testicles.

Farm animals are often neutered so that they will gain weight more rapidly and become more placid. Cats as well as dogs usually have similar reactions, but not to the same degree. Neutering cats can reduce the impulse to wander and fight, especially in males, making these cats better house pets. Tomcats (males) also lose their strong urine odor after castration.

Spaying females prevents unwanted kittens and eliminates gatherings of ardent males around the cat when she is in heat. Generally, neutered cats of both sexes are quieter, stay at home more, and are more attentive to their families.

Chances for diseases of the reproductive organs are eliminated, and the inability to breed means that congenital defects cannot be transmitted.

Because neutered animals are calmer and less active, they have lower caloric needs. Too often owners overfeed their pets and the cats get fat. With proper diet, however, this will not happen.

Neutering is, of course, an irreversible operation, making breeding impossible. If you decide to have your pet neutered, the operation should be done only when the cat is physically mature—has achieved its full size and muscle development. This should be no earlier than eight to ten months, but may not coincide with sexual maturity. In some cases queens are able to have kittens before that age. Consult your veterinarian for specific advice.

In many parts of the country, there are too many unwanted kittens. Most authorities, including this writer, feel that this fact is a compelling reason to neuter. Unless you choose to breed cats, neutering is recommended.

Basic First Aid

Every pet owner should be prepared for emergencies and learn what to do when basic first aid is needed. Injured animals are frightened and in pain. They may be uncooperative, attempt to run away and hide, or be so frantic that they attempt to bite or scratch even a beloved owner. Knowing how to handle the injured cat, wrap it in blankets, or provide other restraining measures can prevent further injury to the patient as well as to yourself. Timely action may be vital.

The most practical first-aid remedy is prevention: Keep your pet under control and away from sources of possible trouble. Freely wandering cats are the most inclined to have problems. The most common accidents in approximate order of frequency include being hit by a car, bite wounds, poisoning (through chemicals or spoiled food), injuries from foreign objects like fishhooks or thorns, falls, cuts, drowning, heat stroke, or injuries as a result of cruelty.

Do you know what to do in an emergency? It is wise to have a book on pet first aid on hand and to be familiar with basic procedures before you need to use these skills. Always keep a simple first-aid kit for pets in your home. It should contain bandages, tape, scissors, a blanket for restraint, and simple medications. These medications should include an antacid laxative such as milk of magnesia; hydrogen peroxide to induce vomiting; antibiotic ointments for the eyes and skin; an antidiarrheal medication such as milk of bismuth or a kaolin and pectin mixture; and mineral oil.

Know the location of the nearest veterinary clinic or hospital. Most metropolitan areas have central emergency or out-of-hours veterinary centers to provide special facilities for injured animals.

The following practical first-aid information tells you what to do in the most common emergency situations until you can get your cat to a veterinarian.

Heat Stroke

When a pet is confined to a poorly ventilated car or a pen that is exposed to the summer sun, it may get heat stroke. The cat may become frantic, be unconscious, or groggy and gasping for breath. Remove the cat from the overheated place at once and immediately wet it thoroughly with water. Dip the cat in a pond, or use a water hose or whatever is handy to soak it all over. Rapid cooling is vital. Then promptly transport the cat to a veterinary hospital for professional treatment.

Poisoning

Cats are commonly poisoned because they groom themselves constantly and can ingest toxic substances picked up on their feet or fur. For example, a cat that walks in antifreeze leaking from a car may lick a lethal amount from its feet. Tar or paint on the hair present similar problems. Never use gasoline or paint solvents to remove it, since these toxic materials are highly irritating to the cat's skin and the cat will inevitably lick them off. Instead, it is best to let the material

harden on the hair and then cut the hair off; it will soon grow back. Cats also like to eat leaves from house plants, but you should try to prevent this because some, like poinsettia, are highly toxic. In cases of suspected poisoning, always seek veterinary advice promptly.

Hair Balls and Swallowed Objects

When cats groom themselves they swallow hair, which can accumulate in the stomach and intestines, causing the cat to vomit. Adding a teaspoonful of mineral oil to the cat's food three days in a row helps compact mats of hair in the stomach and facilitate passage through the intestines. A mild laxative—one to two teaspoonfuls of milk of magnesia—on the fourth day may speed the process. If your cat swallows a small foreign object, it will usually pass safely through the intestinal tract and appear in the stool. To facilitate passage of a sharp object such as a needle, feed your cat small pads of cotton soaked in milk. They will surround the needle and escort it on its journey.

Bleeding

Cuts on the feet or legs are common injuries, which occasionally can cause profuse bleeding. This almost always can be controlled by a firm pressure bandage. In an emergency, pull a clean sock on to the leg or wrap the cut area with a washcloth or layers of paper towels. Then wrap a bandage firmly over the sock or cloth. Start wrapping at the foot and continue up the leg in a spiral, going above the area of the cut. Seek veterinary aid for sutures or better bandaging. (See your first-aid manual for details.)

Removing Fishhooks and Thorns

Deeply embedded thorns and fishhooks require veterinary help, since anesthesia will be necessary. If a fishhook is superficially embedded, try to push the hook through, then cut off the barbed end with cutting pliers and back the hook out. Thorns usually are so deeply embedded that they may be hard to find. If you can locate the thorn, remove it with tweezers and/or a sewing needle. Puncture wounds are always infected, so treatment for this complication is necessary as well.

Fractures and Shock
If a cat falls from a great height or is hit by a car, it will probably have broken bones and may be in shock. Legs with broken bones that are allowed to flop around can produce more serious damage to vital blood vessels, nerves, or tendons in the area of the injury. To immobilize a leg fracture, wrap the leg in thick layers of towel or newspapers that are taped or wrapped with cord to hold them in place. Animals with severe injuries are always in shock. As part of the treatment for this condition they must be wrapped in towels or blankets to conserve heat— even in warm weather—and promptly taken to a veterinary hospital.

Transporting an Injured Cat
To move an injured cat, grasp it by the skin of the neck and by the skin of the rump near the tail. Then gently slide it onto a blanket or into a cardboard box with the side folded down. Pull the cat on the blanket along the ground so that it is moved with the legs trailing behind. Avoid bending the legs or backbone. Once the cat is in the box, wrap blankets around it, keep it warm, and make it comfortable. A closed box or pillow case may have a calming effect. Then carefully lift the box into the car. These measures are easy if the cat is unconscious and not difficult if it is groggy, or knows you well. If the cat is conscious, keep talking to it quietly to reassure it. Be careful in moving the patient so you do not get scratched or bitten. If the cat is really obstreperous, it probably is not too seriously injured; just let it sit or lie in the car as it wishes as you go to the veterinary hospital.

Further Help
The health care suggestions in this section are only an introduction. See your veterinarian for a specific health plan for your cat and for recommendations of books that will provide more detailed information.

Key to Potential Health Problems

Preliminary Checks Before Purchase

For each breed account, the Potential Health Problems section mentions diseases and inherited problems that could affect that breed. Although most cats are quite healthy, certain breeds are more prone than others to some kinds of illness. Before purchasing a cat, it is wise to learn whether your future pet is likely to be susceptible to any serious health difficulties.

Many ailments in cats are not at all serious. Like people, cats are subject to several troublesome but easily treatable maladies as well as health conditions that, while not completely curable, can be managed with medication. To help you evaluate the seriousness of a problem, the chart on the following pages lists common health problems veterinarians find in cats, and rates them according to four categories: treatable ailments, manageable conditions, problems that can be corrected with surgery, and serious problems.

Key to Potential Health Problems

	Treatable Ailments	Manageable Conditions	Corrected with Surgery	Serious Problems
Body Malformations				
Cleft palates			●	●
Face and head abnormalities				●
Kinked tails			●	
Bone Problems				
Crippling arthritis	●			●
Circulatory Problems				
Anemia	●			
Heart defects				●
Ears				
Deafness				●
Eyes				
Cataracts (rare)	●			
Clogged tear ducts	●	●		
Entropion			●	
Glaucoma (rare)	●			●
Lens luxation			●	
Respiratory Problems				
Breathing difficulties caused by short face	●			●
Chronic sinus problems	●			
Skin Problems				
Allergic skin disease		●		
Alopecia		●		
Bacterial skin disease (rare)	●	●		
Other Health Problems				
Urinary incontinence				●

	Treatable Ailments	Manageable Conditions	Corrected with Surgery	Serious Problems
Malformed jaws			●	
Flattened chest (pectus excavatum)		●		●
Spinal deformities (spina bifida)				●
Cardiomyopathy				●
Malformed tear ducts			●	
Ocular dermoids			●	
Retinal dysplasia (rare)				●
Tearing problems	●	●		
Nasal obstruction				●
Upper respiratory infections	●			
Cysts			●	
Seborrhic skin disorders (rare)				●
Skin acne	●			

The Mating Instinct

Should Your Cat Have Kittens?

Veterinarians regularly receive telephone calls from frantic pet owners exclaiming that their cat is dying. She is rolling around on the floor, screaming in pain. Actually, if the cat is a female over five months old, she's probably in heat (estrus)—and she will be in heat, rolling and crying much of the time until she is either bred or spayed. If she has kittens, she will be back in heat as soon as they are weaned.

Female cats, called queens, are amazing in their capacity to reproduce. If it were up to them, they would have three litters per year. At an average of four kittens per litter, the numbers soon become staggering—and explain why millions of unwanted cats and kittens are abandoned annually or put to death in animal shelters.

This is a major reason why cat owners should think long and hard before allowing their pets to breed. Unless the cat is a valuable purebred and the kittens will be part of a planned breeding program, each pregnancy only contributes to the tragedy of animal overpopulation.

Another reason to neuter or spay a cat is that it will make the animal a far better pet. A male cat sprays vertical surfaces such as walls and chairs with strong-smelling urine and can make a home virtually uninhabitable in short order. He may howl, pace, and become aggressive if deprived of a female. If he goes outdoors, he will fight with other tomcats, risking torn ears and scratched eyes. A female cat, besides being noisy, is likely to become irritable and even forget her litter-box training when she is in season. Both males and females are too distracted by sexual urges to be enjoyable companions to their owners.

Selective Breeding

Even if the female is an excellent purebred, breeding her often turns into more of a project than the owner might have expected. Cat breeding can be thrilling and fun—but it is also expensive, exhausting, and often disappointing. Think carefully about all the ramifications, including whether or not there is a market for purebred kittens in your area.

If you do decide that your female is a good example of her breed and you would like to try raising a litter, you will first have to find an appropriate stud cat. Many established breeders do not want the hassle of keeping a male or accepting visiting females, so unless the breed is a common one, you might have to go hundreds of miles away for stud service.

The breeder may want to see the female's pedigree and photographs, and may inquire about her show wins. Do not be offended: Stud owners have a right to be selective about which queens to accept, because the quality of the resulting kittens will reflect on their male as much as on your female. Very few, if any, people are in cat breeding to make a profit; rather, their main goal is to produce the best cats possible.

Since male cats prefer to breed in their own territory, the female is almost always taken to the male's residence. You have a right and responsibility to inquire about what kind of quarters would be available for your female, how many other cats are in the household, whether there have been any recent health problems, and whether the breeder routinely tests for feline leukemia. It would not be out of line to ask for references, since you will be entrusting your cherished pet to a virtual stranger. Also, inquire if the stud will be bred to other queens around the same time. The stud could pass on a vaginal infection from one female to the next if he is bred to more than one queen within a seven-day period.

Assuming the owner of the stud has been

in the breeding business for a while, he or she should be able to evaluate how the bloodlines might blend. It could be that the male and female are too closely related, or perhaps their lines are both noted for the same fault. If such is the case, look elsewhere for a male with strong points that will compensate for the female's weak points, and vice versa. No cat is perfect: The aim should be to compensate for imperfections through selective breeding.

Once the match has been agreed upon, the breeder will estimate when the female cat will come into heat again, based on her previous heat cycles. The stud owner probably will want a health certificate to accompany the cat at breeding time.

Stud Fees and Written Contracts

Purebred stud fees generally start at about $100 and range up to several hundred dollars, depending on the male's record as a show cat and sire. It is important that a signed contract govern the complete transaction, since many complications can and frequently do occur. The female may be so upset at the strange surroundings that she immediately goes out of heat. She may conceive, be sent home to her owner, and abort her litter. Or she may give birth to stillborn or deformed kittens. Both parties involved must have a clear understanding in writing of how the stud fee would be handled in each case. Usually the stud owner either allows a repeat breeding or gives a partial refund if the female does not produce live kittens.

Sometimes the stud owner may request the "pick of the litter" instead of a cash payment. This is a very sticky arrangement, and the newcomer is advised to stay clear of it. What if there is only one kitten? What if one kitten is truly outstanding and the rest are only mediocre? In either case, the queen's

owner would have been far better off paying cash. Why risk giving up a $500 kitten to avoid paying a $200 stud fee?

Care of the Pregnant Female

Once the female is pregnant, she will need very little extra care until the due date, about nine weeks after conception. Do not administer any vaccine or medication during her pregnancy unless prescribed by a veterinarian. Give her a balanced vitamin/mineral supplement but resist her demands for huge amounts of food. Otherwise she will get fat, and an overweight queen has more difficulty giving birth. (Later, when the queen is nursing kittens, she can eat to her heart's content.)

A pregnant queen does need exercise, but she should not be allowed to jump from high places during the last couple of weeks before the kittens are due. Prepare a roomy box for her about a week before delivery and line it with layers of newspapers and soft cloths.

Restlessness is the first sign of approaching labor. The female will wander around the house, go in and out of her box, and dig furiously at its contents. Then, after several hours, she will assume a squatting position; you should be able to see the strong contractions along her sides. Some queens cry or yell when delivering, and others never make a sound.

Guiding the New Mother

Cats usually are good mothers and tend to their necessary duties, such as breaking the umbilical cord, without help. However, a first-time mother needs to be watched closely because she may not know what to do right away. She might expel the kitten and then walk away, not realizing it is alive and needs her care. If this happens, gently bring her back to the box and show her the kitten until she notices it is moving and takes an interest.

If the queen fails to break the sac around

the kitten's head within about a minute after delivery, you must do it so that the kitten can begin breathing. Just tear the membrane with your fingers and peel it back from the kitten's face. The kitten soon will give a welcoming cry to the world, and the mother should take over from there. Soon she will be cuddling her new family as the youngsters enjoy their first breakfast. When she seems to be through delivering, quietly remove the soiled materials and replace them with soft, fresh bedding. The queen may be thirsty, so offer her a bowl of evaporated milk mixed with warm water. Sometime within the next twenty-four hours, you should take the queen to the veterinarian, who will examine her to make sure there are no remaining fetuses. The veterinarian probably will also give her a shot to expel any retained afterbirth, which otherwise could cause an infection.

The Stress of Recurrent Heats

What if you are not quite ready for kittens yet but think you might want to breed your female someday? Unfortunately, female cats cannot be put "on hold" for two or three years. They come in season often and if they are not bred, their hormone system quickly gets out of whack. Recurrent heats are severely stressful to the cat and make her vulnerable to problems such as cystic ovaries, uterine infection, and personality disorders.

Research is under way, but at this time there is no safe or completely reliable method of feline birth control on the market. So unless you are willing and able to cope with litters of kittens on a regular basis, it is best to have the female spayed. Both you and your cat will be happier.

Raising a Kitten

The First Weeks

Kittens, like infants, are born totally helpless. During their first few weeks of life they depend not just on their mother's care, but also on the practical consideration of their owner. A basic grasp of a kitten's various stages of development will help you to better understand and anticipate its needs as it grows. With care and patience, you can ensure that your kitten will mature into a healthy, contented adult.

At birth, kittens must be kept warm and away from drafts. Kittens cannot compensate for lost body heat, and a chill could quickly cause a newborn to go into shock.

A newborn kitten spends nearly all of its time nursing or sleeping. During the first week of life its sense of smell, taste, and hearing begin to develop. In the second week, its eyes, which are tightly shut at birth, will open and begin to focus clearly. All kittens are born with blue eyes, but as they mature the eye color changes.

During the third and fourth weeks kittens cut their baby teeth. Eyesight improves greatly, and as kittens begin to notice their surroundings, they will start to play and toddle around on wobbly legs.

At five and six weeks, kittens jump and play more robustly, and you can notice different personalities emerging. They may begin to nibble food from their mother's dish, and the mother will teach them to use the litter box.

Getting Used to People

Kittens enter an important learning stage at seven and eight weeks. They need daily attention from people to develop good social behavior. Expose them to normal household noises and play with them two or three times a day for ten to fifteen minutes at a stretch (beware of overtiring them). Kittens should be picked up, spoken to softly, and gently petted. At this stage of development, the more they are exposed to kind attention, the more affectionate and outgoing they will become.

By the end of eight weeks, kittens should be weaned and have a healthy appetite for solid food. At this critical time, kittens begin to lose the antibodies provided by the mother's milk; they are very susceptible to colds or digestive upsets and should be vaccinated promptly.

Before moving to a new home—which ideally they should not do before ten to twelve weeks of age—kittens should be fully vaccinated and completely adjusted to a solid diet.

Feeding

Kittens require high-protein, high-calorie food two or three times daily. However, do not overfeed; a fat kitten is not necessarily a healthier one, and may become overweight as an adult if its diet is not properly controlled.

As kittens grow into adulthood, you can decrease the number of meals per day; adult cats require only about half the amount of food kittens need. Serve food at room temperature and always provide clean, fresh water. (For more detailed information, see the essay Health Care.)

Litter-box Training

Mother cats usually teach kittens to use the litter box, but you can reinforce this training by placing the kitten in the box after feeding or playing. Repeat this several times until the kitten catches on. Encouragement is especially important for a kitten that has recently been separated from its mother and introduced to a new home. (For more information, see the essay Problem Solving.)

Socializing Your Kitten

You have a strong influence on the development of your kitten's personality. Temperament is greatly determined by genetic factors, but environment is also significant. Kittens deprived of human attention will naturally be fearful of people and household situations.

It is perfectly safe to begin handling kittens from the time they are born. Picking up a kitten twice a day to check it for proper temperature and weight is an important first step in forming a bond. When handling a kitten, slip one hand under its chest, holding the front legs with your fingers. At the same time, support the hind legs with your other hand. Never pick up a kitten by the scruff of the neck or by the legs. Mishandling can be painful and can rapidly turn a docile animal into a defensive and unfriendly pet.

Even the youngest kitten may hiss and spit at you until it becomes accustomed to your touch. But by the time a kitten's senses have developed fully, human companionship will be a normal and appreciated part of its life. If you acquire a kitten from a breeder or a previous owner, let its first day in your home be a quiet one. Suppress your enthusiasm and allow your new pet time to acquaint itself with the sights and sounds of its new environment. Don't force yourself on your new kitten; let it come to you. Approach it gently and speak in soothing tones. Loud noise or quick movement may startle it and send it rushing under the sofa. The key to forming a lifelong friendship is making the new cat feel secure and loved.

Playing Games

By the time kittens are weaned they will welcome you as a fellow playmate. Ping-Pong balls or small rubber balls become favorite toys, especially if you toss them across the floor a few times to give kittens the idea. A shoe box to hop in and out of provides endless fun. In a darkened room, shine a flashlight on the floor; kittens love to chase the beam back and forth.

Children and kittens can become the best of friends. But be sure you take the time to teach your children that kittens can be hurt if played with too roughly. Contrary to popular belief, kittens do not always land on their feet! Very young children should play with a small kitten only when supervised. Always allow the kitten to slip away for a "cat nap" when it has had enough. As the kitten gets older, playtimes can be increased in frequency and length.

Early Behavior Training

An obedient cat is not born, but made. Behavior that is endearing in a kitten—such as chewing on your fingers or jumping for your hands—quickly becomes irritating and even dangerous as a cat matures. You must teach a cat to respect your rules at an early age.

A kitten, like any other animal, learns by association and repetition. Patience and praise work wonders in teaching a kitten desirable behavior; physical punishment is cruel, detrimental, and ineffective. A cat should never be spanked, especially a young kitten. As a disciplinary measure, a firm "No" with a wave of the hand in the kitten's direction will deliver the message. A kitten reacts to the tone of the voice rather than the words spoken.

If punished immediately—for instance, with a spray of water from a squirt gun —a kitten will quickly associate its bad behavior with an undesired experience. Your response to bad behavior must be immediate and consistent: Punishing a kitten for something that happened ten minutes ago will do no good because the animal will not understand and might eventually become fearful of you.

Each kitten reacts somewhat differently to treatment, so let kindness, patience, and consistency guide you. A kitten raised in a secure environment by a loving owner will become an unfaltering, lifelong companion.

Grooming and Routine Care

Coat Care

All cats will benefit from grooming, regardless of the length of their coat. Although the longhair breeds require daily attention, the shorthair varieties will also certainly benefit from a good brushing twice a week. Most cats shed their coat to some extent in spring and fall, but dry heat in winter as well as sickness or stress also can cause a cat to "drop coat." Grooming the cat during the shedding season will help to remove the dead hair. It will also lessen the risk of hair balls, which can form in the cat's stomach and intestines if it swallows hair when licking or grooming itself.

Start regular grooming when the kitten is first acquired, and you can make it both a habit and an enjoyable experience for the two of you. Being a creature of habit, your cat will soon look for this treatment, going to the same place at the same time each day. On the other hand, if the coat is neglected and the fur is tangled, grooming will be an unpleasant experience for the cat and it will disappear when grooming time is near. Before you use any kind of grooming tool, try it out first on the inside of your forearm. If it scratches or hurts you, replace it.

Grooming Longhair Cats

Assemble all your grooming tools: a good steel comb that has teeth of two sizes, a fine-toothed or flea comb, nail clippers, a grooming brush made with natural bristle rather than nylon, and grooming powder (baby powder or fine French chalk).

Before starting to groom, run your fingers through the entire coat. The cat will enjoy this sensation and will relax. In this way you can also check to see if there are problem areas, such as tangles or oily spots. Then run the wide-toothed section of the steel comb lightly through the fur from head to tail. Comb under the chin and chest; lastly, comb the stomach, the inside of the legs, and under the tail. The latter areas are very sensitive in all cats, so lighten the pressure on the comb. If the coat is free of tangles, you can switch to the finer teeth on the comb and groom again in the same way. Repeat the process, combing every inch of the cat and being sure that the comb is going through the entire coat and not just the top layer. Up to this point, all the hair is combed down.

The next step is to comb the ruff forward and up around the head to form an "Elizabethan collar." The sides of the body are combed up and outward, and the tail is feathered. To do this, hold the extreme tip of the tail, and with short quick strokes fluff the tail fur lightly away from the body so that it forms a good brush. Occasionally, add a light sprinkling of fine baby powder over the whole coat and brush it in the opposite direction from which it grows. This will help the coat stand off away from the body for a truly professional look. Then use a small-toothed or flea comb for the fine fur around the face and ears, again combing forward carefully toward the nose.

If for some reason the coat has become badly matted, the only answer is to take the cat to the vet, who can give it a tranquilizer—or, in very bad cases, an anesthetic—and clip the cat down to the skin. If this happens, as soon as the coat starts to grow again, immediately begin daily grooming sessions.

At the end of grooming, the coats of darker-colored cats—black, red, and tortoiseshell—will be enhanced by a little bay rum hair-dressing liquid. Put a little on your hands and touch lightly down the back and sides. It will bring a nice shine to the coat.

Special Problems of Longhair Cats

One of the problems facing the owners of longhair cats is the occasional incidence of feces clinging to the hair under the tail. If the cat is not to be shown, it is easiest to keep this area clipped short. However, for the show cat, it is a matter of washing the feces off immediately; or, if the soiled area is small, as an emergency measure it can be powdered and when dry, combed out. This procedure is a part of owning a longhair cat and must be accepted as a portion of the essential grooming. Kittens particularly must be watched carefully, since they can easily sit in a soiled litter pan and receive a "pancake." If this is not cleaned off quickly, the anus can become blocked, and serious and painful problems may result.

Keep in mind that if you really don't like grooming longhair cats, you can either keep your cat clipped short or get a shorthair breed.

Grooming Shorthair Cats

Even though shorthairs do not require as much coat care as the longhair breeds, they also need regular grooming. To groom most shorthairs, a fine-toothed or flea comb will remove most of the dead hair. Occasionally, use a rubber grooming brush—but with care. Although it will remove dead hair very well, any prolonged or heavy use of this type of brush can also remove the good hair and may leave bare patches.

All the shorthair breeds will appreciate hand-grooming, and it is probably the most effective method of removing dead hair. Stand the cat on a table and stroke the animal briskly from head to tail with your bare hands, one over the other. For Siamese, Oriental Shorthairs, Colorpoint Shorthairs, and Burmese, finish off the grooming with a rubdown. Use a silk glove or chamois; this causes some static in the coat and will help it cling tightly to the body. The other shorthair breeds will enjoy a light brushing with a soft brush to complete their grooming.

Grooming Kittens

It is especially important to groom kittens daily, particularly longhairs, because often their coat is of a cottony texture that mats and tangles very easily, literally overnight. Small knots may be loosened with the fingers and, as a last resort, clipped out carefully with round-tipped scissors. However, if your pet is a show-type kitten, you will not want clumps of fur missing.

The kitten will quickly become accustomed to being combed and brushed while lying on your lap, or you may find it more comfortable to stand your pet on a table with a towel beneath it to prevent the animal from slipping.

Preparing for the Bath

Many of the shorthair breeds require only occasional bathing, but cats with long or semi-long hair can pick up dust and dirt and are more inclined to develop a greasy coat.

There are many shampoos and conditioners that will enhance the different coat textures in the various breeds. For example, cats with very short, close-lying coats, such as the Siamese and Burmese, will not need a shampoo to give coats body. However, the shorthair breeds with more resilience to their coats, such as the Exotic Shorthair and the Manx, and any of the longhairs, will benefit from shampooing. Each cat will have its own special needs in coat care, and it is wise to try out various shampoo brands to see how the coat will react. Usually, for shorthairs that need it, bathing should be done several days before the cat show in order to allow the natural oils in the coat to return. This group includes the household pet classes of cat, too, since there are many different coat lengths and textures, and each will benefit from a good bathing.

It is relatively simple to bathe a cat. First, assemble all your grooming equipment, plus shampoo, conditioning rinse or white vinegar, two large bath towels, a washcloth, and a hair dryer—the quieter the better.

Before you start the bath, clip the claws on all four feet, being careful to remove only the very tip of the claw. You will see that a vein runs through the claw; it will be most painful for the cat if you cut it. Wash the cat's face first before the bath, cleansing the eyes and inside the outer ear with a washcloth wrung out in a mixture of warm water to which a little "no-tears" baby shampoo has been added. Rinse by wiping several times with warm water only. If a medicated or flea shampoo is used, a small amount of Vaseline or mineral oil should be put in the cat's eyes as a precaution. Dry the face with a towel and proceed with the bath.

The Bathing Procedure

Half fill the laundry tub or sink with warm water. Then, holding the cat's two front feet in one hand and supporting the body with the other hand, gently lower the cat into the water. Many cats are afraid of the sounds of water rather than the water itself, so avoid unnecessary splashing. You may find that the cat will feel more secure if it stands with its front feet over the edge of the tub.

Wet the coat thoroughly all over, except the face, being careful not to get water in the eyes or ears. Remove the cat from the sink and stand it on a small table or counter top. Next, apply the shampoo and work the lather through the coat. If the coat is really dirty or greasy, it may be necessary to repeat the shampoo. Rinse thoroughly, using a sink hose or by pouring cups of water over the coat. Be sure to remove all traces of shampoo or the coat will be dull when dry. If a conditioning additive is to be used—such as cream rinse or white vinegar—dilute it first with warm water for easier distribution. Rinse again until the coat

is squeaky clean, then gently squeeze out the excess water and wrap the cat in a large bath towel. Blot the coat with a towel and do not rub, since this will tangle the coat of a longhair cat. Change towels and blot dry again.

Before using a hair dryer, first test the temperature on your arm. A medium heat is usually best. Then holding the hair dryer about a foot away, keep it moving over the cat as you start to dry the coat, being careful not to blow air in the cat's face and ears. Using the wide-toothed end of the comb for longhair cats, flip the hair up and out from the body as it dries. Don't forget the undersides; if the entire coat is not combed out as you dry the animal, the coat will become kinky and curly. Some cats may not tolerate the dryer; in that case, warm up the bathroom and keep the cat confined there until it is completely dry, combing periodically. Keep the cat out of drafts. It can take up to twenty-four hours for a full-coated cat to dry completely.

For white cats and others that have white in their coat patterns, mix a little laundry bluing powder with the shampoo, proceed as above, and rinse thoroughly. This will bring a bright sparkle to the coat. Be sure, however, that you mix the bluing with the shampoo, not with the cream rinse, or you will end up with a blue cat!

Greasy Coats

For coats that are extremely greasy, a mechanic's hand soap may be used with care. Since this kind of soap contains lanolin, it will leave the coat soft in addition to removing the grease. Start with a well-combed cat, free of tangles. Apply the hand soap a little at a time and work carefully through the unwashed coat. Work it down to the skin with the fingers, giving special attention to the extra greasy spots. Do not put any soap on the cat's face, and if it is used around the ears, be particularly careful that when it is rinsed off none goes near the face. Do not leave it on for more than a few minutes, and do not leave the cat unattended. It can be dangerous if the cat licks this soap. Rinse the coat well with lots of warm water. Then apply the usual shampoo and follow the rest of the bathing procedure.

Ears

After the bath, check the ears to see that they are dry and that there is no sign of dark, crumbly residue, since this could be a sign of ear mites and would necessitate a visit to the vet. Clean the ears with a cotton swab but do not go deeply into the ear, since this can cause damage.

Base of Tail

At the base of the tail, there is often a greasy area that, if not treated, can turn into a condition called "stud tail." It does not, however, only affect male cats. On white or light-colored cats, it is an obviously discolored section, with the hair separating. Stud tail is easily treated with a cosmetic astringent, a gentle detergent, or even medicated soap. Cleanse the skin and then rinse thoroughly. Dry cleaners or powders can also be used for "spot" cleaning.

Stains

White cats can quickly develop yellow stains and may require extra attention. It's better to clean the problem areas daily than to have a buildup of stain that can be difficult to remove. The areas around and under the eyes, which sometimes become stained from tearing, can be cleaned by washing the cat's face with a damp cloth, especially just after the cat has eaten.

Other areas to watch are the front paws and the bib area, where yellowing can be caused by saliva stains. Many breeders of white Persians use baby bibs when feeding their cats to protect the animals' long fur. The front paws may be rubbed gently with cornstarch to absorb the stain, then brushed off. You should pay regular attention to urine stains under the tail, especially on male cats, to prevent a stain buildup.

For stubborn stains, make a paste of cornstarch and peroxide. Leave it on the stain for five minutes, being careful not to get any of the paste near the eyes and nose. Wash the cat off and dry it. (Note: The peroxide will have a drying effect on the coat if it is used too frequently.) New pet products are now available in the form of a powder to replace this homemade remedy.

Flea Shampoos

It is essential to keep your pet's coat free from fleas and other parasites, and an occasional bath with a good flea shampoo may be necessary. Be sure that the medicated or flea shampoo is safe for cats. Many of the shampoos made for dogs contain material harmful to cats, so read the label or buy from a veterinarian.

Diet

An important part of routine cat care is a correct diet. A cat's general condition is reflected in its appearance, and no cat can look its best unless it is receiving a well-balanced diet that includes adequate vitamins and minerals.

The Well-Balanced Cat

Cleanliness, exercise, and lots of loving care are necessary to the physically and temperamentally well-balanced cat. Good care includes a regular health check by a veterinarian. The mouth should be checked routinely for signs of tooth or gum disease and buildup of tartar. Vaccinations should be kept up-to-date with regular booster shots.

Problem Solving

Encouraging Good Behavior

Cats do not like to be bossed around. They are proud, independent creatures with wills of their own. Nag a cat for doing something naughty, and it is likely to toss its head and dance away with a devilish gleam in its eye. True cat lovers delight in the animal's free spirit and spunky attitude. If you want a pet that will obey a set of laid-down rules, probably a cat is not your best choice.

Does this mean that cat owners have to give up all semblance of control and completely turn over their homes to their pets? Are people expected to calmly watch their couches and drapes shredded by sharp claws, houseplants chomped to pieces, yards of toilet paper pulled from room to room?

No! You can prevent improper behavior in your cats if you go about it the right way, using a bit of feline psychology and a lot of human ingenuity.

Using Psychology

First of all, understand that force simply does not work with cats. Physical punishment will only offend the cat and make it distrust and dislike you. This is particularly true if the punishment comes more than a few seconds after the offense has occurred. There is no way you can explain to a cat that you are slapping its flank because of something it did twenty minutes ago. Constant scolding every time the cat does something wrong does not work, either, and gradually will sour what should be a happy, loving relationship with your pet.

Some people keep a plant sprayer handy and squirt water at an offending cat. This may have some effect, but only if it is done at the instant the cat misbehaves, every time it misbehaves, and anonymously—that is, so the cat associates the water with its own action and not with your being there.

A far more reliable and less time-consuming answer can be found by outwitting the cat through pre-emptive planning. Rather than punishing bad behavior after it happens, anticipate trouble and head it off. Instead of angrily shooing your pet off the dinner table, feed the cat well before you sit down to eat so that it will curl up and snooze during your meal. Instead of yelling when your cat chews on an electrical cord, coat the cord with Bitter Apple jelly, an awful-tasting product available in pet stores; one good mouthful should cure this dangerous habit. Rather than wailing at the sight of toilet paper strewn throughout the house, reverse the roll so that the paper comes out from the bottom; then when the cat twirls the roll, normally in the other direction, nothing will happen. To avoid finding a half-eaten fern, hang your plants out of reach.

Keep in mind, however, that you will end up with a very frustrated cat if its instincts and energies are not allowed some kind of release. The trick is to rechannel those impulses along acceptable lines. For example, give your cat a bout of strenuous exercise just before you go out so that it will sleep while you're gone and not get into mischief. One excellent way to do this is to tie a string or cord to the end of a pole, put a bow on the end of the string, and flick it around the room. The cat will race and leap wildly as it tries to catch the soaring "bird."

Preventing Destructive Scratching

The specter of ruined furniture and drapes turns many people against cats. No doubt about it, sharp little claws can do big damage to a home. This is indeed a serious problem for cat owners. The cat does not set out to be mean or destructive, but scratching objects is an important part of the feline's strong instinct for self-grooming—in this case, grooming the claws. Cats condition their claws by catching the outer, worn part on a rough surface and drawing it through the material until the old claw flakes off, exposing the new claw underneath.

Today many people have a quick answer to the problem: Get the veterinarian to remove the cat's front claws. Although this is a common procedure, it is extremely controversial—heatedly debated among cat lovers—and should never be approached lightly. Declawing deprives the cat of a crucial defense against harm. A declawed cat must never be allowed outdoors, since it would be helpless against dogs and could not climb trees, as cats normally do, to escape danger. Some people believe that declawing can lead to biting, insecurity, shyness, and/or loss of litter-box training.

Yet some cat owners feel the operation is worth it if the only alternative is to give up the cat. If you do opt for declawing, it should be done early—as young as three months—and you should seek out the most reputable, competent veterinarian you can find, because the cat will truly suffer if the operation is not done well. One good method is to contact a local cat club and find out which veterinarian the cat breeders recommend.

As an alternative to declawing, a cat's claws can be trimmed so that even if it does scratch where it shouldn't, it won't cause as much damage. Use clippers for human nails or trimmers specially designed for pets, but be careful not to cut into the pink part of the claw or it will bleed.

Scratching Posts

A scratching post also can help protect your home against damage from claws. If you give the cat its own property to scratch, something even more enticing than your couch, it may well leave your furniture alone.

Many people do not like scratching posts because they bought one at the pet store and watched it topple over the first time their cat tried to use it. Naturally this would turn both the owner and the cat against scratching posts. The fact is, most commercial scratching posts are not big enough or sturdy enough for an adult cat, but you can easily and inexpensively make your own. Simply cover a board with carpeting and nail it to a wall, making sure it is high enough for a fully stretched cat. You could also cover and mount a thirty-inch pine board on a two-foot-square heavy wooden base. Even a fireplace log with bark on it will work. Sprinkle catnip on the scratching board, post, or log and encourage the cat to use it by gently moving its paws in a scratching motion while murmuring words of praise. Meanwhile, discourage the cat from going near the furniture by covering it with cloths sprayed with cat repellent or mothballs stuffed into old nylon stockings. If you go out, leave the cat in a room with the scratching post but no vulnerable furniture. Soon the cat will get in the habit of scratching only the post.

If all else fails, consider investing in furniture that does not appeal to cats, such as heavy vinyl; or, you may prefer the cheaper alternative of covering torn furniture with an attractive throw.

House Soiling

Mother cats almost invariably train their kittens to use the litter box before they are old enough to wean. It is not a difficult task, because cats are fastidious by nature. So why do house pets sometimes forget to use the litter box or stop using it altogether?

House soiling probably causes more cats to be put to sleep than any other behavioral problem. Before taking such a drastic step, however, the cat owner should look for other solutions. Obviously something is wrong, and the owner has a responsibility to do everything possible to identify and correct the problem.

There are many reasons why a cat might lapse from its toilet training. One particularly dangerous reason is cystitis, a bladder infection that is more likely to strike males than females. Symptoms include leaving small amounts of urine around the house, blood in the urine, frequent urination, or straining over the litter box with no results. If urinary blockage occurs, the cat can die within hours—so it is essential to get it to the veterinarian fast.

If the cat is an adult male, he is quite likely to spray urine against vertical surfaces such as walls. This is normal, instinctive behavior to mark territory and attract females. In most cases, the spraying will stop within a few weeks if not immediately once the male is neutered. If he is to be used for breeding, he will have to be confined to an easily cleaned area where his strong-smelling spray will not cause permanent damage to the home. Females in heat often spray, too, for similar reasons.

Some cats will refuse to use their litter box if it is not clean enough. Removing the stool with a scooper twice a day, and washing the box and refilling it with fresh litter once a week, should solve that problem.

The box may be too small or too flimsy for the cat to use comfortably. It may not be in a private enough location to suit the cat's dignity. It may be in an inconvenient location, such as in the basement, when the cat spends most of its time in a second-floor bedroom. It may be too close to the cat's food dish. A change of litter brand can prove unsettling. Or the cat may object to sharing its box with another cat. Some cats have a habit of just missing the box; others dig so vigorously that they send litter flying around the room. In both cases, the solution is a covered litter box.

Emotional factors, such as a new cat or a new baby in the house or leaving the cat alone too long, may make it feel insecure or resentful and lead to house soiling. Try to ease the animal's anxieties by giving it extra attention and support. If the disruption is only temporary, perhaps a veterinarian can prescribe tranquilizers. If the problem will be long-range, the cat might be happier in a carefully chosen new home.

Elderly cats may have trouble moving around, and occasionally they may not make it to the litter box in time. Try to be understanding and place the box where the cat can get to it easily.

If a cat has had an "accident" in an inappropriate place, it is crucial to remove all evidence or the cat will be attracted to that place again. Soiled areas should be cleaned as thoroughly as possible and sprayed with either a cat repellent or odor counteractant, both available in pet stores. As an added precaution, perhaps the spot can be covered with something such as a chair or a lamp.

Safety

Even if a cat never goes outdoors, it faces a myriad of potential hazards in the home. To prevent tragedy, always think defensively where your cat is concerned. Remember that the famous feline curiosity often gets cats into trouble. Leave a door open even for a second, and your cat is likely to climb into the refrigerator, freezer, or kitchen cabinets to investigate. Play it safe: Always check on where your cat is before leaving home or going to bed for the night.

Also, keep in mind that kittens and cats are likely to swallow anything they can get in their mouths. Keep them away from potential hazards: pins, nails, paper clips, thread, string, rubber bands, Christmas tree needles, tinsel, aluminum foil, foam rubber, plastic bags, medicines, poisons, harsh cleansers, and poultry or pork-chop bones that splinter. Rocking chairs can mangle a paw. A slammed door can break a tail. A cat grabbing a swinging cord can pull a hot iron down on itself. A kitten can drown in a toilet on which the cover was left open.

Many houseplants are toxic. Indoor cats looking for something to do might decide to munch on them with tragic results. If plant poisoning should occur, the cat requires immediate veterinary attention or it could die. Your veterinarian can tell you whether your favorite plant is dangerous to your cat. If it is, either hang it out of reach or spray it regularly with a bad-tasting liquid such as pepper solution or vinegar.

A lot of heartbreak could be avoided if people got in the habit of asking themselves, "Could this possibly hurt the cat?"

Feeding Difficulties

Finicky cats generally are made, not born. With an occasional exception, kittens that are weaned on a variety of foods will grow up to accept most anything put before them. Food preferences generally are fixed, for good or ill, by the time a kitten is a few months old. However, it is very easy to spoil a cat. When the cat is slow to eat its meal, perhaps because it is not all that hungry right then, do not take up the dish and then prepare another, more enticing meal. A cat is smart enough to realize quickly that if it just holds out a bit, it will get something better, and you will have a full-blown finicky feline. The way to keep your cat's appetite perky is to leave meals down for only about fifteen minutes, then take any uneaten food away. Do not offer any more food until the next regular meal, twelve hours later if you feed twice daily. Above all, do not give in. The cat soon will catch on that it must eat promptly or go hungry. Of course, if the cat does

not eat for more than twenty-four hours and seems depressed, a trip to the veterinarian is in order.

If a cat is accustomed to one type of food and you want to switch to another, do it gradually unless the cat takes to the new food right away. Start out by mixing one part of the new food to four parts of the old, then slowly increase the proportion of new food. At each step, wait until the cat thoroughly enjoys the mixture before going on to the next step.

Make sure to feed your cat a balanced, high-quality diet. Surprisingly, an unbalanced diet, even if it tastes good, can cause loss of appetite. Veterinarians are a good source of information, although they disagree on some issues such as the feeding of raw meat or whether vitamin supplements are advisable.

A cat may have trouble chewing due to a problem with its teeth, which a veterinarian can remedy. It may be intimidated by another, more dominant cat and not get its fair share, in which case the cats should be fed separately. Or it may bolt its food, causing vomiting, in which case it should be fed small meals more frequently. If a cat is too fat or too thin, a veterinarian can put it on a proper diet and/or treat what could be a related health problem.

Hair Balls

Cats love to keep themselves clean by licking their fur. Much to the owner's dismay, a frequent result is a matted hair ball thrown up on the carpet. Hair balls form in the cat's stomach as the fur accumulates from self-grooming. The condition is rarely fatal, but it can be uncomfortable for the cat and sometimes can lead to digestive complications requiring veterinary treatment.

A dry cough, constipation, and loss of appetite are common signs that a cat has a hair ball. Once the cat vomits a tubular mass of fur, usually several inches long, the problem is solved for the time being. Unless preventive measures are taken, however, it will recur again and again. The best way to combat hair balls is to comb or brush the cat daily to get rid of the loose hair. This is particularly important in the spring, when cats normally shed their winter coats. Also, longhair cats need more grooming because they have a larger volume of hair to eliminate.

Another precaution is to give the cat regular doses of some commercial product that works as an internal lubricant to prevent hair balls from forming. Such products are available in pet stores, and most cats enjoy the taste.

Bedding

Many cat owners spend a fortune on fancy baskets for their pets to sleep in, then discover the cat prefers to sleep on its master's bed. Given a choice, most cats will snuggle up with their owners at night. They enjoy the warmth and the closeness.

Some people decide, however, that they would sleep better without sharing the bed. In preparing a special bed for a cat, look for a warm place, free of drafts and preferably off the floor. Cats frequently seek high places to snooze, perhaps because heat rises and the location offers protection. An elevated, out-of-the-way nook or cranny can be perfect for a cat bed.

Choose a bed that can be washed or at least wiped clean, such as a wicker basket. A cardboard box does not meet this requirement but can be easily replaced as necessary. Cats love softness, so line the bed with some kind of soft cloth. Most cats absolutely adore the round, furry cat beds with a roll several inches high around the edge. They curl up in the middle and relish the security of being protected on all sides. These beds, which can be thrown in the washing machine and dryer, are sold at

cat shows and in pet stores. It is a good idea to buy one for each cat in the household or they will constantly vie for it.

Traveling with a Cat

If you do not want to leave your cat behind when you travel, it is often possible to take it with you. A cat can be transported quite easily by automobile or airplane, but cats are banned from interstate bus lines and Amtrak trains. Cruise ships, even if they accept pets, may require that they be kept in a separate kennel area.

When traveling by car, a carrier or large cage provides both security for the cat and safety for the driver. A loose cat's antics could seriously distract the driver, causing an accident. Carriers and cages are available in any pet store. For longer trips, a cage is better because it can accommodate both the animal's bed and litter box.

Before a long trip, it helps to take the cat on a couple of short rides around town to see how it reacts and to get it accustomed to the car. On the big day, refrain from feeding the cat for several hours before departure so that it won't get an upset stomach en route. Always remember to take along all the cat's necessities—litter box, litter, scooper, food, bowls, toys, and water (like people, many cats are sensitive to changes in water).

Never leave a cat shut in a parked car when the sun is shining. Temperatures in the car can rise to more than 120 degrees in just a few minutes, causing brain damage or death from heat stroke. Many if not most motels allow pets, but it's a good idea to check ahead. While at the motel, make sure the cat does not escape from the room when the maid comes in to clean.

Cats that travel by air will need an advance reservation, a health certificate from a veterinarian, certain vaccinations, and a well-labeled carrier that meets the airline's specifications. Sometimes a cat can travel under the owner's seat; otherwise it will have to ride in the baggage compartment. If at all possible, book a direct flight to minimize trauma for the cat.

Taking a pet to a foreign country can be complicated. Hawaii and Great Britain, for example, require long quarantines; some Caribbean islands do not accept cats at all. Information about foreign restrictions and requirements may be obtained from your veterinarian, an airline, or the embassy of the country to be visited.

Boarding

If you cannot take your cat with you when you travel, the next best thing is to have a trusted friend cat-sit, either in your home or the friend's home. Some cities have professional pet-sitting services, for which you should check references. Always leave detailed instructions about the cat's feeding and care, and telephone numbers where you can be reached.

Sometimes it is necessary to board a cat, a risky proposition even under the best of conditions. The cat that finds itself abandoned, away from home, locked in a small cage, surrounded by strange animals, and not knowing if it will ever see its family again is quite likely to stop eating and become ill. To make the best of the situation, it is imperative to find the most comfortable and conscientious boarding facility available.

Ask your veterinarian for suggestions. Sometimes veterinary clinics have their own boarding areas, which should be isolated from quarters for sick animals. When you get a list of three or four possibilities, visit them personally and check them out. Does the kennel owner require proof of vaccinations before admission? Does the place look and smell clean? Are water dishes fresh? Are there

flies or other insects around? Do the animals seem reasonably alert and relaxed? Is the temperature too hot or too cold? Does every pet get the same diet, or will special requests be honored? Good boarding facilities may be booked up weeks in advance during holiday periods, so make a reservation early. Also, make sure your cat is healthy and up-to-date on its shots. When you drop it off at the kennel, leave telephone numbers in case of emergency.

Letting a Cat Outdoors

Cats, unlike dogs, can live happy and healthy lives without ever going outdoors. Particularly in cities, cats are far safer and live far longer if they are kept inside. If they have never gone out, they do not know what they are missing and are perfectly content to watch the world go by from the windowsill.

By letting a cat roam outdoors, the owner is subjecting it to the risk of accidents, attacks from other animals, traps, theft, poisoning, fleas, ear mites, worms, and contagious diseases such as feline leukemia. Moreover, unaltered males and females that are allowed to wander will contribute to the animal overpopulation problem by breeding frequently.

If a cat does go outdoors, it should wear a safety collar with an elastic insert so that if the collar gets caught on a tree limb or fence, the cat can slip free and not hang itself. The collar also should feature an identification band or tag with the owner's address or telephone number in case the cat gets lost.

Some cat owners build enclosed outdoor runs, which are safer than letting the cat run loose, and/or install a commercial cat door, which lets the cat go in and out of the house at will.

The Hunting Instinct

For centuries, "working cats" have been valued for their ability to keep the mice and rat populations down on ships, farms, and in cities. However, this highly developed hunting instinct often is not so appreciated when the unfortunate target is a songbird, a squirrel, a chipmunk, or a baby rabbit. The fact that a cat kills for fun—not just to appease hunger—offends many people's sensitivities.

Even if kittens never go outdoors and never see a rodent, the instinct is so strong that they will practice their hunting skills for hours on end in play with their littermates. When removed from their playmates, they will stalk and pounce on a toy or any other available object.

When a cat kills a bird or a small animal outdoors, it often deposits the carcass on the doorstep. This probably relates to the practice in the wild of a mother cat bringing home prey for her kittens to eat, or it may be simply that the cat is proud of its triumph and wants to show off to its owner. The cat will be hurt and confused if the owner becomes angry, but it won't lose its natural need to hunt.

The best way to deter an outdoor cat from killing birds is to put a bell on its collar so that the birds have a chance to get away in time. It may prove unwise to place a bird feeder on your property, but if you do have one, be certain that it is well out of a cat's reach. Do not put out rabbit food or similar attractions that might lure other creatures to their deaths.

Introducing a New Cat

Feline introductions should occur slowly. Don't bring a new cat into the house and just throw it together with an older pet. The two animals could very well start fighting and may never become good friends. Your older pet naturally will feel threatened by a newcomer. It helps to give the older cat extra attention so that it will not feel it is being pushed aside. Meanwhile, confine the new cat to a

room by itself where it can relax and get accustomed to the scents and sounds of its new home. At the same time, it will lose its strange smell and gradually acquire the smell of its surroundings, which will make it less objectionable to your older cat when the two pets finally meet.

When your older cat seems to have adjusted to the fact that there is a strange animal in the house and no longer constantly sniffs underneath the door, try letting the newcomer out under your close supervision. Don't leave the cats alone together until you are absolutely sure that they will not get into a squabble.

Adopting a Stray

The act of adopting a cat off the street can be very fulfilling. Often such cats turn out to be the most loving pets of all, because a home offers new-found security and warmth.

Before officially adopting a stray, you should try to find out if the cat is somebody's lost pet. You can check with the humane society, advertise in the "found" section of the newspaper, and perhaps place fliers giving the cat's description around the neighborhood. Taking a stray cat into your home does carry a risk, particularly if you already have a cat. The stray may be suffering from fleas, ear mites, worms, fungus infection, an upper respiratory ailment, or even feline leukemia, which is eventually fatal. Until it has been examined by a veterinarian, the new cat should be isolated from all other pets. The veterinarian should thoroughly examine, test, and vaccinate the stray. Then if everything checks out right, including a blood test and vaccination (if appropriate) for leukemia, the cat can be introduced to other pets in the household.

The veterinarian may announce that the cat is pregnant. In that case, you will

have to consider whether you are willing
to take on the extra responsibility of
raising and finding good homes for the
kittens. If not, the veterinarian can spay
the cat before the kittens are born.
Most strays quickly learn to use a litter
box, but just in case, it is a good idea to
confine the newcomer in a small area
with the box until the habit is clearly
established.

The Older Cat

Indoor cats that have received excellent
nutrition and regular veterinary attention
may live twenty or more years. Although
an older cat may behave like a kitten at
times, it is slowing down and probably
needs more sleeping time. One or more
of its senses—perhaps eyesight or
hearing—may gradually decline, but
most cats adjust well to old age with a
little consideration from their owners.
For example, it would be cruel to
completely rearrange your furniture
when your old friend can no longer see to
get around.

Veterinary checkups every six to twelve
months will help an elderly cat. The
veterinarian can remove tartar buildup
from the teeth, provide medications and
supplements if the cat has difficulty with
digestion or elimination, suggest a diet
if the cat develops a weight problem,
and watch for tumors, arthritis, and
other ailments.

Even though plagued by the infirmities
of aging, a cat can continue to enjoy life
for some time. If a cat is in pain,
however, it will stop eating, become
depressed, and withdraw from household
activities. At that point, the owner must
weigh what the prognosis is and whether
it is fair to allow the cat to continue
suffering. The end of a loving pet is
always heartbreaking, but the owner
should try to make it as peaceful and
comfortable for the cat as possible.

The Cat Registries

A Wide Choice of Organizations

The cat fancy is governed by various associations, each of which sponsors shows, oversees its member cat clubs, and has its own purebred standards and rules concerning registration. The largest and most prominent of these organizations is the Cat Fanciers' Association. For most breeds, the Ideal Appearance section of the breed account is based on the CFA standards; for those breeds that are not accepted for CFA championship status, the Ideal Appearance description represents a summary of the standards of associations registering that particular breed.

Names and Addresses

Listed here are the names and addresses of registries active in North America. For registration information, show rules, and registry standards, contact the association in which you are interested. Some organizations have no permanent headquarters; the addresses given are those of the current secretary, registrar, or president.

American Cat Association (ACA)
Ms. Susie Page, Secretary
10065 Foothill Boulevard
Lake View Terrace, CA 91342

American Cat Council (ACC)
Bettina Hazen, Secretary
1255 E. Badillo, Apt. A
Covina, CA 91724

American Cat Fanciers' Association (ACFA)
Ed Rugenstein, General Manager
P.O. Box 203
Point Lookout, MO 65726

Canadian Cat Association (CCA)
Susan Plant, Office Manager and Registrar
General Office
14 Nelson Street W., Suite 5
Brampton, Ontario, Canada L6X 1B7

The Cat Fanciers' Association, Inc. (CFA)
Thomas Dent, Executive Director
1309 Allaire Avenue
Ocean, NJ 07712

Cat Fanciers' Federation (CFF)
Dr. Margery Collier, President
9509 Montgomery Road
Cincinnati, OH 45242

Crown Cat Fanciers' Federation (CCFF)
4106 Muhammad Ali Boulevard
Louisville, KY 40212

The International Cat Association (TICA)
Leslie Bowers, Executive Director
P.O. Box 2988
Harlingen, TX 78551

United Cat Federation (UCF)
Jean Ford, Recorder
6616 E. Hereford Drive
Los Angeles, CA 90022

Showing Your Cat

How to Enter

Whether your cat is a purebred or a household pet of mixed or unknown ancestry, entering it in a cat show is enjoyable and rewarding.

Forthcoming shows are listed in the various publications of the cat fancy, notably the *Cat Fanciers' Association Almanac* and *Cats Magazine*. To enter a show, you must contact the show secretary or entry clerk of the sponsoring cat club at least one month before the show date, and request an entry form and show information sheet. Your signature on the completed entry form means that you agree to abide by the association's show rules. A copy of these rules may be obtained from the organization sponsoring the show. Send the entry form with the required fee to the entry clerk. Within a week or so, you should receive an acknowledgment by mail, along with a map and directions to the show's location, and a list of accommodations in the area should you wish to stay overnight.

Preparing Your Cat

To compete, cats must be clean, healthy, and free from fleas, ear mites, and disease. All entries must be vaccinated against feline enteritis, feline rhinotracheitis, and calicivirus. It is also advised that before entry cats and kittens be tested for feline leukemia virus and up to date on shots to prevent the disease. Claws must be trimmed on all four feet (just the very tip, removed with nail clippers). No entry may be declawed.

Classification

To give you an idea of how a cat show works, here is a basic outline of the format used by the Cat Fanciers' Association. Further details can be obtained by contacting the CFA. Guidelines vary among the other organizations; each will provide them on request.

The Cat Fanciers' Association has three main show categories: Championship, Premiership, and Nonchampionship.

Championship

Pedigreed, CFA-registered adult cats compete in this category, which is divided into three classes, each at a higher level than the last. Cats are judged according to breed and, if applicable, by color class within the breed. Cats eight months old or more that have not completed requirements for Championship confirmation are entered in the Open Class. After attaining the required six winner's ribbons under at least four different judges, the cat qualifies for confirmation as a Champion. An owner must obtain confirmation of this status by submitting a championship claim form to the CFA. The cat then competes in the Champion Class. For each other Champion it defeats in a division or the finals, the cat earns one point. A total of 200 points qualifies the cat for the top level of competition, Grand Championship. (As you can see, the cat must be of very high quality to achieve this title.)

Premiership

This category is the counterpart of Championship but is designed for CFA-registered cats eight months old or more that have been neutered or spayed. The class divisions are Open, Premier, and Grand Premier. Progression from level to level is parallel to that in the Championship category except that only 75 points are required to become a Grand Premier, since the field of competition is smaller.

Nonchampionship

This category consists of five classes. To compete in the Kitten Class, kittens must be four to eight months old on the opening day of the show and, except for their age, must otherwise be eligible to compete in the Championship category. Awards are given in color classes but there are no breed or winner's ribbons. Kittens compete only with other kittens for final awards.

The AOV (Any Other Variety) Class includes CFA-registered cats or kittens that by pedigree are entitled to Championship but that do not, on the basis of color, coat, or other physical feature, conform to the written show standard.

The Provisional Breed Class includes registered cats or kittens of a breed that has a written standard accepted by the CFA but is not recognized for Championship status. Finally, as the last pedigreed group, the Miscellaneous Class consists of registered cats or kittens of a breed not yet accepted as Provisional.

The Household Pet Class consists of nonpedigreed, domestic cats or kittens of unknown or mixed ancestry in all varieties of colors, patterns, and coat lengths. These cats are judged strictly on health, beauty, and temperament. There is no written standard and the judge may choose whichever cats he or she pleases for the finals. The Household Pet Class is always a very popular part of the cat show and draws large crowds.

Finals

At the end of the judging in the various categories, the top ten cats in each ring are chosen and awarded appropriate rosettes. In most shows, for the Kitten, Premiership, and Household Pet classes, the top five cats are chosen, but in large shows the top ten receive awards.

At the Show

Plan to arrive at the show room at least one hour before judging is due to start so that you will have ample time to check in and prepare the cat's cage. The show secretary, who is usually located close to the entrance, will ask to see your entry confirmation so that your cat can be marked as present for the show. The secretary will assign your cat a number, for which there is a corresponding

cage in the show room. Its use is included in the price of the entry fee. The size of a single cage is usually about $24'' \times 24'' \times 24''$; however, if your cat is large or needs more room, for an additional fee you may order a double cage ($24'' \times 24'' \times 48''$) when you submit the entry form.

Preparing the Cage

Once you have located your cat's cage in the show room you can begin to prepare it. Pin up a set of drapes or colorful towels inside the cage. This will give your cat privacy from the cats benched on either side and also makes the cage more attractive. Cover the floor with another towel or small blanket. If you have a male cat that sprays, it is wise to drape the cage in plastic for cleanliness. Some clubs provide exhibitors with disposable litter boxes for the cages, but it is advisable to bring a small one with you in case none is supplied. A small water dish will complete the cage. When all is ready, place your cat in the show cage and store the carrier under the table. Bring cats and kittens to the show room only in a suitably roomy, well-ventilated carrying case, never wrapped in a towel or on a leash. Your cat should settle down for the day. Be sure to have its favorite food with you, but don't be surprised if the cat does not eat—it will be too busy looking around, especially if this is its first show. If your cat is frightened by the strange sounds or other distractions, talk to it and reassure it. There are a few common-sense rules that every exhibitor should heed. Among the most important are these two: Never touch a cat that does not belong to you without the specific permission of the owner; and never feed someone else's cat, even if you think it looks hungry. Be sure that you are familiar with all the show rules and comply with them. They are made for your protection and for your cat's welfare.

Reviewing the Show Catalog

Once your cat is comfortably settled, buy a show catalog from the club's committee and study it carefully. Every cat and kitten entered in the show will be listed in the catalog, and for registered purebreds, will include all the pertinent information: the entry's name and registration number, date of birth, sire, dam, breeder's name, and owner's name. This information is not necessary for household pets. If your cat is purebred and registered, check to see that all the details appear in the catalog exactly as they are listed on your registration certificate. It is important that this be correct, or wins can be lost. To make corrections, notify the show secretary immediately, and request the master clerk to make the correction in the official catalog that is sent to the sponsoring association at the end of the show.

The catalog will also contain the order of judging in each of the rings. Most shows have four rings, each with a different judge who handles all the entries in his or her ring. However, some clubs now hold six- or even eight-ring shows. (The more rings, the higher the entry fee.)

Judging Procedure

Once the show gets under way, pay close attention to all announcements. You will note that the judging ring consists of numbered cages placed on tables. When the announcer calls your cat's number, take your cat to the judging ring, place it in the cage bearing the corresponding number, and close the door carefully. Do not speak to the judge; take a seat and watch the judging procedure.

The judge stands behind a table that is covered with plastic or another washable material. A clerk assists the judge with the clerical duties and a steward cleans each cage immediately after it has been vacated. One at a time the judge removes a cat from its cage, places it on the table, and examines it carefully. Expert hands check the bone structure, length of tail, color, condition, and length of coat, eye shape and color, ear set, muscular condition, and—most important—the overall balance of the cat. Purebred registered cats and kittens are judged against a written standard for each breed that has been approved and accepted by the association sponsoring the show. Watching each judge at work will help you learn about and appreciate the different breeds and colors. After returning the cat to the judging cage, the judge disinfects his hands and the table area. This helps prevent the spread of any disease and also deodorizes. (Many cats dislike even the slightest odor left by another cat.) When the judge has completed examining the class, he or she will award the ribbons and then dismiss the cats. Collect your cat and return it to its own cage, holding it securely.

Finals

At the end of all the judging in each class, each ring will hold "Finals." This is one of the most exciting parts of the show, especially if your cat is one of those chosen as a finalist. Be sure to listen to all the numbers that are called, and go to the judging ring to check which cats have been called back. In some show halls, the announcements are not always clear, so watch the show schedule carefully so that you will know when certain classes are being judged. It is important to take your cat to the ring promptly when called or it will be marked absent. These procedures may seem confusing the first time around, but if you are in doubt about anything, don't hesitate to ask fellow exhibitors for help and advice.

Exhibitors' cats are required to remain in the show room during the advertised hours of the show. One reason for this is to allow the spectators, who pay admission to the show, to see all the exhibits. You can be proud to have your cat admired along with all the other entries. If it is a two-day show, you must return on the second day before the judging begins.

When the Exhibition Ends

If you stay at a hotel overnight, be sure your cat is well behaved. Some hotels refuse to accept pets because of previous experience with thoughtless owners. You are liable to be held responsible for damage caused by your cat. Take newspaper with you to put under the food and water dishes and the litter box, placing them carefully in the bathroom. Leave the room odor-free, being certain to dispose of all litter and trash in a bag. Likewise, in the show room when the exhibition is over, leave your cat's cage area clean and tidy.

By the end of the show you will find that you have made new friends and learned about many breeds of cats. Win or lose, chances are that you will have caught enough of the excitement to want to attend another show soon.

Cat Show Checklist

Make a checklist of items you may need to take to the show and have them ready the day before so that in the excitement of preparing to leave, you do not overlook anything important. Such items include:

Entry confirmation
Cat's health certificate (required in some states)
Copy of show rules
Hotel confirmation
Directions to show room
Drapes and floor covering for cage
Litter box
Food and water dishes
Cat food, can opener, knife, spoon
Grooming tools
Nail clippers
Paper towels
Tissues
Small garbage bag
Sandwich or snack food
Cat in its carrier

Body Language

Hidden Messages

Are you able to translate the subtle signals of body language your cat sends? Is there special meaning in the rhythmic movement of the tail or the insouciant flip of an ear? While people ponder the significance of crossed or uncrossed arms and legs, cats send us highly synthesized information with every movement. They have perfected the art of body language.

The Contented Cat

Who could mistake the aura of contentment portrayed by a gently curved sleeping cat? The relaxed posture of the cat reflects a complete harmony with secure, familiar surroundings. In fact, society has accepted the image of a sleeping cat as a synonym for home and hearth. Whether rounded tightly into a ball or stretched out upside down in the middle of the floor, the peace and contentment that the cat exudes is obvious. A cat can even stretch deeply, all the way down to its toes, without disturbing its state of tranquility.

As a cat awakens, it uses even more body language to convey information. Signs of a relaxed state are the heavy-lidded blinking of the eyes or the careless twitch of a whisker. Some breeds have unique rituals of relaxation that portray at very special times. A Manx or a Cymric, for example, will extend the front legs together in a lazy stretch, then the hind legs in a synchronized movement. This "one-two" Manx/Cymric stretch is never performed unless the cat is completely at ease and content. Sometimes such a cat will display this trait—the ultimate show attitude—on the judging table, to the delight of both the audience and the judge.

Yawning is another signal that measures the cat's state of relaxation. A long, slow, wide-mouthed yawn, showing lots of teeth and pink tongue, signifies that the cat feels safe and secure. An uptight cat will always be alert.

Changes in Mood

From a deeply relaxed sleeping position to a quiet standing posture, the cat is able to exhibit marked changes. Monitor your cat as you use an electric can opener or open a refrigerator door. Are the ears perked? Do the eyes follow your every movement? Should the cat decide to underscore a need for nourishment, it will putter (or thunder) to the kitchen, persistently dipping and rubbing against your legs as it competes for your full attention. Occasionally, it will perform a full body stretch, gently touching with its paw as high as it can reach. This motion will be repeated, nonchalantly of course, until the message is not only received but acted upon.

Reaction varies from cat to cat, but many breeds act almost predictably at dinnertime. Place a plate of delectable morsels before a Burmese and you might well receive an indifferent "What, again?" reaction; a Siamese, however, might knock you over en route to the food.

Many cats clearly demonstrate apprehension when placed in strange, unfamiliar surroundings. A high degree of apprehension is indicated by a tense, frozen posture, usually in a dark, hidden cranny. A cat in a state of great agitation will not investigate, but will sprint and hide until it feels more secure. Once it no longer feels threatened by the unknown, it will inspect every aspect of its quarters.

Although the eyes of a cat are both bright as a video screen and veiled in mystery to the uninitiated, the most apparent barometer of mood is the cat's tail. A happy, relaxed cat waves its tail like a Fourth of July flag. An intent, interested cat will carry its tail straight up, like a ship at full sail. An angry cat whips its tail back and forth in strong, defiant strokes. A startled, fearful cat will distend each hair until the tail resembles a bottle brush. Momentary uncertainty may cause only the hair at the base of the tail to rise and separate. For kittens, the soft twitching of a mother cat's tail can become a prize trophy to seize and capture, as they vie with one another in endless variations of the seek-and-stalk game.

Body Signals

Ears can be a major clue to a cat's mood. Tense, flattened ears indicate anger, fear, or displeasure. Pricked, alert ears signal that the cat's computer is turned to "on." It has been theorized that the larger the cat's ear, the keener is its ability to hear. The large-eared Siamese or Oriental cat is normally quick and enthusiastic in its response, whereas a small-eared breed such as Persian or Himalayan is more likely to present an aura of studied indifference.

The legs and paws are used to actively coax, touch, and strike. The cat may explore tentatively or playfully everything from a man's beard to a dripping water faucet. Leg movements are swift and precise when used to inhibit or to stake a claim. It is hard to misunderstand the intent to warn or threaten when a cat rapidly extends its leg and distends its claws. This body language shouts a message of "Hands off!"

Consider the typical Halloween black cat image. The legs are stiff and unyielding, and the body is arched in fear. The ears are upright and alert, and each hair of the cat's coat stands out as if individually frozen. This posture is as clearly a signal of distress as the soft "kneading" rotation of the front feet is an indication of happiness and contentment.

Sexual Language

Both the male and female cat have stylized scripts that signal their sexual interest. A female will become restless and then more vocal. Suddenly every piece of furniture becomes an object of interest as she rubs against it. At the height of estrus, or heat, she will display a tightly arched body and slowly rotating hindquarters, and her tail will conveniently flip to the side.

A male has less overt symptoms of sexual excitement. His strongest message is spraying, which consists of a backing motion and a shaking of the tail. Neutered males will sometimes go through these motions but are not as likely to actually spray, or mark with scent, their "territory."

Self-Expression

Indeed cats use body language to reveal a rainbow of colorful emotions. Watch your cat carefully and begin to appreciate and observe the statements it makes. Cats have a highly developed system of communication, and they use all parts of their body to express themselves. They are programmed by habit to respond in a highly predictable manner. Learn to tune in to the special frequency of cats and develop a more complete relationship with your feline companion.

Understanding Color Genetics

A Sex-linked Characteristic

Coat color in cats is sex-linked and appears only on the X chromosome. Because a female cat has two X chromosomes, it can show two equally dominant colors at one time, and thus, many multicolor patterns are possible, such as tortoiseshell consisting of red and black, or blue-cream with patches of both blue and cream. However, the male cat normally has one X and one Y chromosome and thus can show only one color at a time.

Much experimentation and genetic research has been possible based solely on inherited color traits. Not only can breeders predict the coat color resulting from a mating, but by applying basic genetic principles, they are able to create new colors.

Many purebred cats have been produced in new colors that at first were not registerable or accepted for show. For example, all the cameo colors were developed in the early 1950s by crossing silver, smoke, and tortoiseshell cats, but these hues were not recognized as championship colors until 1961. New colors and patterns are continually being developed.

Basic Coat Color Theory

Because color is sex-linked, cats with multicolor patterns are usually female. For example, since the female cat has two X chromosomes, it can carry black on one and red on the other; this pattern, called tortoiseshell, shows both black and red splotches in the coat. When an abnormal male occurs with an XXY chromosomal makeup, it can carry two different colors on the two X chromosomes, and thus be a tortoiseshell. However, this genetic makeup is rare and such males are almost always sterile.

Not only is color limited to the X chromosome, but there are actually only two colors—black and red, which

scientists call eumelanin and phaeomelanin. All of the other colors and patterns come from genetic modifications either in the pigment or in the way the colors appear on each individual hair. None of these modifications is sex-linked.

Some modifications in color pigment result from the presence (or absence) of a diluting gene. Two possible alterations in individual hair pigmentation are an agouti pattern, in which each individual hair has bands of color (as seen in Abyssinian colors or tabby patterns), or a nonagouti pattern, in which each hair is a single color and not banded (as seen in any solid color cat). A cream tabby is really a red that has been affected by both a dilution gene and the agouti gene. Blue-smoke is a black that has been affected by both the dilution gene and the shaded (tipping) gene.

The Special Case of White

White is not actually considered a color, because it functions as a masking gene. A white cat may be "masking" a red or a black gene in addition to any number of possible alteration genes, which can be traced by studying the cat's color pedigree and its progeny. In a calico cat, white functions as a partial mask, appearing as white with black and red splotches.

Because coat mutants are inherited independently from color, each type of coat—longhair, shorthair, wirehair, or hairless—is theoretically possible in every color variety.

A Multitude of Colors

Today the Cat Fanciers' Association recognizes over one hundred colors and patterns of purebred cats. The Color Glossary describes each color in detail.

Color Glossary

Cats exist in a wide variety of colors and patterns. Many of these colors and patterns are the same for a large number of breeds, and thus can be defined in terms that apply to most breeds. On the following pages, the color and pattern descriptions are divided into five groups: solid colors, particolors, shaded (tipped) colors, point-restricted colors, and tabby patterns and colors. Within each division, the color definitions are arranged alphabetically. To help you visualize these groups, the chart on pages 22–23 illustrates examples of each color division.

Certain breeds have unique colors that occur only in those breeds. These colors and patterns are described in the Special Breeds Color Glossary. Each breed is listed alphabetically with definitions of its special colors and patterns.

All descriptions are based on the colors and patterns presently accepted for championship status by the Cat Fanciers' Association in America, but they are not intended to duplicate actual show standards. Despite some variations, the colors and patterns accepted by other registries are essentially the same as those described here.

Solid Colors
A single overall shade from the roots to the tips.

Particolors
Two or more distinct colors.

Shaded (Tipped) Colors
Coat appears to be single shade but has a light-colored undercoat with a darker color on the hair tips.

Point Restricted Colors
The points—mask, ears, legs, feet, and tail—are a dark color that contrasts with a light body color. This is typically called a Siamese or Himalayan-type pattern.

Tabby Patterns and Colors
Complex patterns usually consisting of stripes in at least two colors.

Special Breeds Color Glossary
The following breeds have unique colors: Abyssinian, Birman, Bombay, British Shorthair, Burmese, Devon Rex, Egyptian Mau, Havana Brown, Japanese Bobtail, Korat, Malayan, Oriental Shorthair, Russian Blue, Somali, Tonkinese.

Solid Colors

A single overall shade from the roots to the tips.

Black
Dense coal-black. Nose leather and paw pads black or very dark brown. Copper or gold eyes. Kittens are born black but often develop smoky undercoat, ruff, and/or rust-colored tips before they become solid colored as adults. Show faults: rust on tips and smoky or lighter-colored undercoat.

Blue
Actually gray, varying from pale bluish gray to almost steel blue-gray. In most breeds lighter shades preferred. Nose leather and paw pads steel-gray. Copper or gold eyes.

Chestnut
Synonym for Chocolate, but nose leather and paw pads slightly lighter cinnamon shade.

Chocolate
Warm, rich shade of chocolate-brown. Nose leather and paw pads brown. Copper or gold eyes. Show faults: lighter brown undercoat, shading, or tabby markings.

Cream
Buff colored to light beige. Palest color —almost whipped cream—preferred. Nose leather and paw pads pink. Copper or gold eyes. Show faults: reddish shading on back and lighter undercoat (faulty color is called "Hot Cream").

Ebony
Synonym for Black.

Lavender
Frosty gray with pinkish hue, similar to Lilac.

Lilac
Much lighter than Blue. Very pale lavender with pinkish or mauve tone. Nose leather and paw pads pink. Copper or gold eyes. Show faults: any bars or stripes.

Red
Deep, rich red ranging from dark orange to almost Irish Setter mahogany. Same color overall, including lips and chin. Nose leather and paw pads brick-red, not pink. Copper or gold eyes. Show faults: tabby markings.

White
Pure white. Nose leather and paw pads pink. Three eye types: blue-eyed cats (deep blue); copper-eyed cats (copper or gold); and odd-eyed cats (one blue and one copper or gold eye). Kittens often born with dark-colored spot on back of head that gradually disappears as cat matures. Show faults: yellowing, tipping, or any other color showing on coat.

Particolors

Two or more distinct colors. Light-colored blaze on face highly desirable. Bicolor cats, including Van Bicolor, can be male or female, but all other particolors are only female.

Bicolor
White with large patches of one other solid color, either black, blue, red, or cream. White must be on muzzle, chest, undersides, legs, and feet, but at least 50 percent of body should be colored. White under tail and around collar allowed. Inverted white V blaze on face desirable. Nose leather and paw pads pink. Copper or gold eyes.

Blue-Cream
Dilute form of Tortoiseshell. Basically pale gray with large, clearly defined patches of pale cream. In most breeds, palest shades of both blue and cream preferred. Large cream blaze on face highly desirable. Nose leather and paw pads blue and/or pink. Copper or gold eyes. Show faults: tabby markings.

Blue-Cream and White
Same as Dilute Calico.

Calico
Tortoiseshell and White, with white predominating on underparts and legs. Large, clearly defined patches of red, black, and usually cream should cover at least 50 percent of body. Nose leather and paw pads pink and/or black. Copper or gold eyes. Show faults: brindling (streaking).

Dilute Calico
Blue-Cream and White combination, with white predominating on underparts and legs. Large, clearly defined patches of blue and cream. Nose leather and paw pads blue and/or pink. Copper or gold eyes. Show faults: tabby markings.

Tortoiseshell (Tortie)
Black, with large, clearly defined patches of red and cream. Blaze of red or cream on face and at least three red or cream

toes highly desirable. Nose leather and paw pads black or pink-and-black splotched. Copper or gold eyes. Show faults: bars, brindling (streaking), or lighter color undercoat.

Tortoiseshell and White
Same as Calico.

Van Bicolor
Mostly white bicolor with clearly defined patches of black, blue, red, or cream on face, legs, and tail. One or two small color patches allowed on body. Nose leather and paw pads correspond to surrounding coat color. Copper or gold eyes. Show faults: brindling (streaking).

Van Blue-Cream and White (Van Dilute Calico)
Basically white with clearly defined patches of blue and cream on face, legs, and tail. Nose leather and paw pads blue and/or pink. Copper or gold eyes. Show faults: brindling (streaking).

Van Calico
Basically white with clearly defined patches of black and red on face, legs, and tail. One or two small colored patches allowed on body. Nose leather and paw pads black and/or pink. Show faults: stripes or brindling (streaking).

Shaded (Tipped) Colors

Coat appears to be a single shade but has a light-colored undercoat with a darker color on the hair tips.

Black Smoke
Appears black at rest, but when hair is parted shows pure white undercoat, very deeply tipped with jet-black. Ruff and ear tufts white. White undercoat should be clearly visible on forehead when black-tipped hairs are parted. Nose leather and paw pads black. Copper or gold eyes. Show faults: bluish cast to undercoat and ruff or any slate-gray tipping.
Black Smoke kittens are born solid jet-black, with no white undercoat; they have silvery raccoonlike markings around eyes and silvery hairs on legs; begin to develop white undercoats when about one month old. If Black Smoke kitten is born with any visible white undercoat, its adult color will not be deeply tipped enough for show.

Blue-Cream Smoke
Dilute form of Tortoiseshell Smoke. Appears blue-cream at rest, but when hair is parted shows pure white undercoat deeply tipped with blue and cream patches. Large cream blaze on face and at least three cream toes desirable. Ruff and ear tufts pure white without any smoky cast. Nose leather and paw pads blue and/or pink. Copper or gold eyes. Blue-Cream Smoke cats are always female.

Blue Smoke
Dilute form of Black Smoke. Appears gray-blue at rest, but when hair is parted shows pure white undercoat deeply tipped with blue. Ruff and ear tufts pure white, not bluish. Nose leather and paw pads steel-gray. Copper or gold eyes.

Cameo Smoke (Red Smoke)
Appears red at rest, but when hair is parted shows pure white undercoat deeply tipped with bright red. Ruff and ear tufts pure white. Nose leather and paw pads brick or rose. Copper or gold eyes. Show faults: cream undercoat, brownish tipping, or tabby markings.

Tortoiseshell Smoke (Smoke Tortie)
Appears to be Tortoiseshell except for white ruff and ear tufts. When hair is parted, shows white undercoat deeply tipped with black, red, and cream patches. Red or cream blaze on face and at least three red or cream toes desirable. Nose leather and paw pads black and/or pink. Copper or gold eyes. Show faults: tabby markings and grayish undercoat. Tortoiseshell Smoke cats are always female.

Chinchilla (Chinchilla Silver)
Undercoat pure white. Back, tail, flanks, and head very delicately tipped with black. Ruff, ear tufts, chin, chest, legs, and stomach pure white with no tipping. Rims of eyes, lips, and nose outlined with black. Nose leather brick-red. Pad pads black or charcoal colored without any pink. Green or blue-green eyes.

Chinchilla Golden
Undercoat is rich, warm cream, almost apricot in color. Chin, ear tufts, chest, ruff, and stomach should be same apricot color but are often lighter shades of cream. Back, flanks, head, legs, and tail delicately tipped with black. Nose leather rose or brick colored. Paw pads black. Rims of eyes, lips, and nose outlined with black. Green or blue-green eyes. Show faults: black stripes or bars on legs or tabby markings on body.

Shell Cameo (Red Chinchilla)
Appears pale pink if next to solid white cat. Undercoat pure white with delicate red tipping on back and upper parts of head and tail. Chin, ear tufts, ruff, chest, stomach, and under tail white; legs mostly white. Nose leather and paw pads rose colored. Copper or gold eyes. Show faults: cream or brownish tipping.

Shell Tortoiseshell (Shell Tortie)
Pure white undercoat with delicately tipped patches of black, red, and cream on top of head, back, tail, and upper legs. Chin, ear tufts, ruff, chest, stomach, and under tail pure white. Red or cream blaze on face and at least three red or cream toes desirable. Nose leather and paw pads black and/or pink. Copper or gold eyes. Shell Tortoiseshell cats are always female.

Shaded Cameo (Red Shaded)
Much redder than Shell Cameo. Undercoat pure white. Ruff, chest, ear tufts, stomach, and under tail white with no tipping. Face, back, flanks, sides, legs, and tail evenly tipped with bright orange-red. Nose leather and paw pads brick-red or rose. Copper or gold eyes. Show faults: cream tipping or tabby markings.

Shaded Golden
Rich apricot-colored undercoat with deeper black tipping from back to sides, and on flanks, legs, tail, and face than Chinchilla Golden. Nose leather brick-red or rose. Paw pads black. Eyes, nose, and lips outlined with black. Green or blue-green eyes. Show faults: tabby markings.

Shaded Silver
Much darker than Chinchilla Silver. Undercoat pure white. Chin, ruff, chest, stomach, and under tail white with no tipping. Delicate black tipping on face, legs, tail, and down sides of body. Nose leather brick-red. Paw pads black. Eyes, nose, and lips outlined with black. Green or blue-green eyes.

Shaded Tortoiseshell (Shaded Tortie)
Undercoat pure white, not in the least grayish. Top of head, back, down flanks, upper legs, and tail tipped with patches of black, red, and cream. Red or cream blaze on face and at least three red or cream toes are desirable. Chin, ruff, ear tufts, stomach, and under tail pure white without tipping. Nose leather and paw pads black and/or pink. Copper or gold eyes. Show faults: tabby markings. Shaded Tortoiseshell cats are always female.

Point Restricted Colors

The points—mask, ears, legs, feet, and tail—are a dark color that contrasts with a light body color. All points should be of the same shade (or combination of shades in some breeds). The mask covers the entire face, including the whisker pads, and is connected to the ears by definite tracings; it should not extend over the top of the head. Show faults: usually no white hairs allowed on points. All pointed cats have vivid blue eyes. Pointed kittens are usually born white or off-white and gradually develop darker point colors as they mature. Body color should remain light and even, but in some darker colors, subtle shadings are allowed in mature cats. Pointed cats generally darken with age, but points should never lose their obvious contrast with the body.

Solid Color Points
Points are a single, solid color in contrast to lighter body color.

Blue Point
Body cold-toned, very pale bluish white, shading gradually to pure white on stomach and chest. Points deep blue. Nose leather and paw pads slate-blue.

Chocolate Point
Lighter, but along the same brown tones as Seal Point. Body pale ivory, without darker shadings. Points warm, rich milk-chocolate.

Cream Point
Dilute form of Flame Point, but lighter overall. Body pure white with a warm, creamish cast. Points buff-cream tone, dark enough to contrast with body but not dark enough to approach an apricot or reddish tone. Nose leather and paw pads pink. Show faults: shading on body.

Flame (Red) Point
Body warm cream-white with slight shading allowed, but pure white on chest and stomach. Points deep orange or brilliant red. Nose leather and paw pads brick-red, not pink.

Lilac Point
Much lighter than Blue Point. Body pure, glacial white. Points pale, frosty gray with a pinkish tone in certain lights. Nose leather and paw pads pink. Show faults: shading on body.

Seal Point
Body even pale fawn to cream color, gradually shading into an even lighter shade on chest and stomach. Points deep seal-brown. Nose leather and paw pads same color as points.

Particolor Points

Points are two or more colors in contrast to lighter body color. In some colors, a light-colored blaze is very desirable. Particolor points are always female.

Blue-Cream Point

Body cold-toned, bluish white to platinum-gray, shading to much lighter color on chest and stomach. Points deep blue-gray, uniformly mottled with cream, not red. Nose leather and paw pads blue with pink mottling.

Chocolate-Tortie Point

Body warm ivory with some mottling in older cats. Points warm milk-chocolate, uniformly mottled with red and/or cream. Blaze of red or cream on face highly desirable. Nose leather and paw pads cinnamon with coral-pink mottling.

Lilac-Cream Point

Extremely delicate impression. Body pure glacial white without darker shadings, except on older cats. Points frosty gray, with almost pinkish cast in certain lights, and uniformly mottled with cream. Cream blaze on face highly desirable. Nose leather and paw pads lavender pink with light pink mottling.

Seal-Tortie Point

Body pale fawn to cream, shading to even lighter color on chest and stomach; may be mottled with cream in older cats. Points deep seal-brown uniformly mottled with red and/or cream. A red or cream blaze on face highly desirable. Nose and paw pads seal brown with coral-pink mottling.

Tortie Point

Same as Seal-Tortie Point.

Lynx-Pattern Points

Points are thick bars against ground color that is light enough to show bars clearly, but not so light as to appear the same shade as body. Dark-colored ears should show a lighter-colored thumbprint in center. Body is very light, but as cat gets older, ghost markings may show a tabby striping.

Blue-Lynx Point

Body pale bluish-white, shading to pure white on chest and stomach. Points barred with deep blue. Nose leather and paw pads slate-gray.

Chocolate-Lynx Point

Body pale ivory. Points barred with chocolate. Nose leather and paw pads brown.

Flame (Red)-Lynx Point

Body warm cream-white, shading to pure white on chest and stomach. Points barred with deep orange or brilliant red. Nose leather and paw pads flesh or coral-pink.

Lilac-Lynx Point

Body glacial white. Points barred with pale, frosty gray. Nose leather and paw pads pink.

Seal-Lynx Point

Body an even pale fawn to cream color, shading to lighter hue on chest and stomach. Points barred with deep seal-brown. Nose leather and paw pads seal-brown.

Tabby Patterns

Complex patterns usually consisting of stripes in at least two colors.

Classic Tabby Pattern
A complex pattern of broad, well-defined markings in a much deeper hue than ground color. Legs are ringed with dark bracelets. Neck and upper chest have several unbroken necklaces. Entire tail has even, dark rings. Forehead has upward-pointing lines that form the letter M. A broad stripe runs down spine, flanked on either side by a narrow line. These three dark stripes are well separated by stripes of ground color. Cheeks have swirls; an unbroken line runs from eyes onto cheeks. Shoulder has a dark butterfly or saddle design. Each side displays identical bull's eye, formed by a blotch of dark color surrounded by one or more rings. Stomach and chest have double rows of buttons or dark spots.

Mackerel Tabby Pattern
A complex pattern of narrow, well-defined markings in a much deeper hue than ground color. All markings are much narrower than those of Classic Tabby, and there is no bull's eye on either side. Legs are ringed with narrow bracelets. Body markings are narrow pencilings, which run completely around body. Like Classic Tabby, Mackerel Tabby pattern has rings around tail, M on forehead, and stripes down spine, but with narrower lines.

Patched Tabby Pattern (Torbie Pattern)
Classic Tabby or Mackerel Tabby pattern only in silver, brown, or blue with random patches of red and/or cream throughout coat. Red or cream blaze on face is desirable. Patched Tabby cats are always female.

Spotted Tabby Pattern
See Special Breeds Color Glossary.

Ticked Tabby Pattern
See Special Breeds Color Glossary.

Tabby Colors

The basic tabby patterns come in the following colors:

Blue-Patched Tabby (Blue Torbie)
Pale bluish-ivory ground color with deep blue markings in Classic Tabby or Mackerel Tabby pattern and clearly defined cream-colored patches on body and extremities. Nose leather and paw pads blue and/or pink. Copper or gold eyes.

Blue Tabby
Pale bluish-ivory ground color, including lips and chin. Very deep blue (but not black) markings in either Classic Tabby or Mackerel Tabby pattern should be in distinct contrast with much paler ground color. Usually has warm fawn overtones or patina. Nose leather and paw pads faded pink or color of old roses. Copper or gold eyes.

Brown-Patched Tabby (Brown Torbie)
Copper-brown ground color with jet-black markings in Classic Tabby or Mackerel Tabby pattern and clearly defined random red and/or cream patches on body and extremities. Nose leather and paw pads black with pink areas. Copper or gold eyes.

Brown Tabby
Rich copper-brown ground color with very dense jet-black markings in Classic Tabby or Mackerel Tabby pattern. Back of legs black from paw to heel. Chin and under stomach as dark as rest of ground color, never cream or white. Nose leather brick-red. Paw pads black. Copper or gold eyes.

Cameo Tabby
Pure white ground color with brilliant red-tipped markings in either Classic Tabby or Mackerel Tabby pattern. Shade of tipping varies widely, ranging from shell-cameo-tipped markings to smoke-cameo-tipped markings. In all shades, ground color must be white and markings red with distinct pattern. Nose leather and paw pads rose colored. Copper or gold eyes.

Cream Tabby
Dilute form of Red Tabby. Extremely pale cream ground color with darker cream markings in Classic Tabby or Mackerel Tabby pattern. Nose leather and paw pads pink. Copper or gold eyes. Show faults: red markings.

Patched Tabby and White
See Tabby and White.

Red Tabby
Light red ground color with deep rich mahogany-red markings in Classic Tabby or Mackerel Tabby pattern. Lips and chin red, not cream or white. Nose leather and paw pads brick-red. Copper or gold eyes.

Silver-Patched Tabby (Silver Torbie)
Pale, clear silver ground with black markings in Classic Tabby or Mackerel Tabby pattern and clearly defined red or cream patches on body and extremities. Eyes, lips, and nose outlined with black. Nose leather brick-red. Paw pads black and/or pink. Green, copper, or hazel eyes.

Silver Tabby
Pale, clear silver ground color with distinct dense black markings in Classic Tabby or Mackerel Tabby pattern. Nose brick-red. Paw pads black. Eyes, lips, and nose outlined with black. Green, copper, or hazel eyes.

Tabby and White
Classic Tabby, Mackerel Tabby, or Patched Tabby pattern and any tabby color with pure white chest, muzzle, underside, legs, and feet. White under tail and white collar are allowed. Eye color, nose leather, and paw pads correspond to surrounding coat colors. With addition of white, Tabby and White occurs in all tabby patterns and colors. White blaze on face is desirable.

Special Breeds Color Glossary

Abyssinian
Ticked, or agouti-type, pattern: Each single hair shaft has at least two or three bands of dark color interspersed between lighter bands. In all Abyssinian colors, eyelid skins are dark, encircled by lighter-colored area.

Blue
Warm, soft blue-gray ticked with various shades of deep slate-blue. Extreme outer tip is darkest with almost ivory-colored undercoat. Ticking should never be so dark as to appear black, nor should undercoat, undersides, and chin be so light that they appear white. Nose leather dark pink. Paw pads mauve.

Red
Warm red ticked with chocolate-brown. Deepest red tones preferred. Ears and tail have chocolate-brown tips. Nose leather rosy pink. Paw pads pink, with chocolate-brown between toes, extending slightly beyond paws.

Ruddy
Ruddy brown ticked with various shades of darker brown or black. Extreme outer tip black; undercoat rich apricot to orange-brown. Darker shading along spine allowed if fully ticked. Tail tipped with black. Nose leather tile-red. Paw pads black or brown, with black between toes and extending slightly beyond paws. Gold or green eyes. Show faults: bars on legs or tail. Kittens are born with tabby markings, which gradually disappear.

Birman
Four basic pointed-pattern colors of seal point, blue point, chocolate point, and lilac point. All with white "gloves" on paws. On front paws, white gloves end in an even line across paw at third joint. On back paws, white gloves cover entire paw, which must end in a point, called laces, that goes up back of hock. Deep, vivid blue eyes, the more violet the better. Paw pads pink. Nose leather corresponds to color of points.

Bombay
Solid black to roots. Kittens born lighter brown and darken with age. Nose leather and paw pads black. Gold to copper eyes.

British Shorthair
Only Spotted Tabby pattern unique to breed. Other colors shared with other breeds.

Spotted Tabby Pattern
Body, legs, and tail covered with round, oblong, or rosette-shaped spots. Spots must be dark and distinct against lighter ground color. Very few obvious bars, connected lines, or rings. Classic Tabby markings on head.

Spotted Tabby Colors
Any recognized ground color with appropriate dark spotting is accepted. Silver Tabby and Brown Tabby have black spots. Red Tabby has mahogany-red spots. Nose leather, paw pads, and eyes correspond to those of Classic Tabby hues.

Burmese
Rich, warm, sable-brown, shading almost imperceptibly to lighter hue on underparts. Otherwise without shadings, bars, or markings of any kind. Nose leather and paw pads brown. Eyes range from yellow to gold; the greater the depth and brilliance, the better. See Malayan for the three other CFA Burmese colors.

Devon Rex
Two special patterns. Other colors shared with other breeds.

Spotted Tabby Pattern
Same as Oriental Shorthair.

Spotted Tabby Colors
Silver Tabby and Brown Tabby have black spots. Blue Tabby has blue spots. Red Tabby has deep red spots. Nose leather, paw pads, and eyes correspond to those of Classic Tabby hues.

White Spotting Pattern
White with spots or patches of any
Devon Rex color. Show faults: brindled
(streaked) spots or patches.

Egyptian Mau
Spotted Tabby pattern with body spots
on either side of torso; these do not need
to match, but must be dark and distinct
against lighter ground color. Spots vary
in size and shape. Classic Tabby
markings on head. Heavily ringed tail,
barred legs, and dark dorsal stripe
differentiate this breed from almost non-
barred British Shorthair Spotted Tabby.
Eyes pale gooseberry-green in mature
cats, but amber cast accepted in
adolescents.

Bronze
All spots and bars dark brown. Body
ground color light bronze gradually
fading through tawny-buff to creamy
white on undersides, chest, throat, chin,
and around nostrils. Back of ears tawny-
pink tipped in dark brown. Nose, lips,
and eyes outlined in dark brown. Nose
leather brick-red. Paw pads black or dark
brown with same color between toes and
partially up hind paws.

Silver
All spots and bars dark charcoal. Body
ground color pale silver gradually fading
through very pale silver to almost white
on undersides, chest, throat, chin, and
around nostrils. Back of ears grayish
pink tipped in black. Nose, lips, and
eyes outlined with black. Nose leather
brick-red. Paw pads black, with black
between toes and partially up hind paws.

Smoke
All spots and bars jet-black. Body
ground color consists of silver undercoat
with charcoal-gray tipping. Coat
gradually fades to much lighter silver
shading on undersides, chest, throat,
chin, and around nostrils. Back of ears
smoke tipped with black. Nose, lips,
and eyes outlined in black. Nose leather

and paw pads black, with black between
toes and partially up hind paws.

Havana Brown
Rich, even, dark brown overall,
differentiated from seal or chocolate by
its warm burnt-sienna cast. Kittens often
have ghost tabby markings, which they
lose as adults. Nose leather and paw pads
brown with rosy flush. Whiskers brown.
Vivid green eyes.

Japanese Bobtail
Known for boldly patterned tricolor (*mi-
ke*) females in Calico or Tortoiseshell and
White. Many other colors and patterns
accepted. Nose leather, paw pads, and
eyes should harmonize with coat color.

Korat
Pale silver tipping over silver-blue
ground color. Cat should appear same
color overall with lustrous, almost
iridescent sheen. Nose leather and lips
dark blue or lavender. Paw pads range
from dark blue to lavender-pink. Eyes
green to amber, but green preferred.
Show faults: tabby markings.

Malayan
Three distinct colors. Kittens often
lighter shades and darken as they age.
Eyes range from yellow to gold; the
greater the depth and brilliance, the
better.

Blue
A medium blue with definite fawn-
colored overtones. May be slightly
lighter on underparts. Nose leather and
paw pads slate-gray.

Champagne
Warm honey-beige, gradually shading to
pale gold-tan on underparts. Slightly
darker shades permissible on face and
ears; less shading preferred. Nose leather
light brown. Paw pads pinkish-tan.

Platinum
A pale silver-gray with very pale fawn
overtones. May be slightly lighter on

underbelly. Nose leather and paw pads lavender-pink, perceptibly paler than in the Blue. Show faults: shading or markings.

Oriental Shorthair
Numerous special colors unique to breed in addition to many shared colors. Eyes green, except in solid whites.

Blue-Cream Silver
Similar to Blue-Cream Smoke, but with shallower blue-cream tipping, so creates overall lighter appearance. Nose leather and paw pads blue and/or pink.

Blue Silver
Similar to Blue Smoke, but with shallower blue tipping, so creates overall lighter appearance. Nose leather old rose. Paw pads rose.

Cameo
Same as Shaded Cameo.

Chestnut Silver
Rich chestnut tipping. Pure white undercoat. Nose leather pink. Paw pads cinnamon.

Chestnut Smoke
Deeply tipped with chestnut. Pure white undercoat. Much darker than Chestnut Silver. Nose leather and paw pads lavender-pink.

Chestnut-Tortie
Chestnut-brown with red and/or cream patches.

Chestnut-Tortie Silver
Rich chestnut tipping, mottled or patched with red and/or cream. Pure white undercoat. Nose leather and paw pads cinnamon and/or pink.

Cinnamon
Much lighter than Chestnut, but with same warm tones. Nose leather and paw pads cinnamon.

Cinnamon Silver
Cinnamon tipping. Pure white undercoat. Lighter appearance than

Chestnut Silver. Nose leather pink. Paw pads coral.

Cinnamon Smoke
Deeply tipped with cinnamon. Pure white undercoat. Much darker than Cinnamon Silver. Nose leather cinnamon. Paw pads coral.

Cinnamon-Tortie
Cinnamon with red and/or cream patches.

Cinnamon-Tortie Silver
Cinnamon tipping, mottled or patched with red and/or cream. Pure white undercoat. Lighter appearance than Chestnut-Tortie Silver. Nose leather and paw pads cinnamon and/or pink.

Ebony Silver
Shaded silver with black tipping. Pure white undercoat. Nose leather brick-red. Paw pads black.

Fawn
Pale pinkish-fawn. Nose leather and paw pads pale fawn.

Fawn-Cream
Fawn with cream patches.

Fawn Silver
Fawn tipping. Pure white undercoat. Much lighter appearance than Cinnamon Silver. Nose leather and paw pads pink.

Fawn Smoke
Deeply tipped with fawn. Pure white undercoat. Much darker than Fawn Silver. Nose leather fawn. Paw pads pink.

Lavender-Cream
Lavender with cream patches.

Lavender-Cream Silver
Delicate lavender tipping, mottled or patched with red and/or cream. Pure white undercoat. Nose leather and paw pads lavender and/or pink.

Lavender Silver
Delicate lavender tipping. Pure white

undercoat. Nose leather pink. Paw pads lavender-pink.

Lavender Smoke
Deeply tipped with lavender. Pure white undercoat. Much darker than Lavender Silver. Nose leather and paw pads lavender-pink.

Particolor Smoke
Deeply tipped with either ebony, chestnut, blue, or lavender, patched with red and/or cream. Pure white undercoat. Much darker than silver counterpart of the same tipping color. Nose leather and paw pads appropriate to tipping color.

Tortoiseshell Silver
Any of the Oriental Shorthair shaded colors, mottled or patched with red and/or cream. Pure white undercoat. Nose leather and paw pads appropriate to tipping color.

Spotted Tabby Pattern
Body, legs, and tail covered with round, evenly distributed spots that do not run together in a broken-mackerel pattern. Dark dorsal stripe from shoulder to tip of tail. Classic Tabby markings on head. Legs barred.

Ticked Tabby Pattern
Ticked pattern same as in Abyssinian, but with barring on face, legs, and tail. Some tabby markings on underside.

Tabby Colors
Classic, Mackerel, Spotted, or Ticked tabby patterns may be any of the following colors: blue, blue-silver, cameo, chestnut, chestnut-silver, cinnamon, cinnamon-silver, cream, ebony (brown tabby), fawn, lavender, lavender-silver, red, or silver.
Patched Tabbies with Classic, Mackerel, Spotted, or Ticked tabby patterns may be the following colors: blue, chestnut, ebony, silver, or lavender tabby with patches of red and/or cream. Patched Tabbies are always female.

Russian Blue
Even, pale blue overall, with distinctly silver-tipped outer hairs. Contrast creates a lustrous silvery sheen. Nose leather slate-gray. Paw pads lavender-pink or mauve. Eyes vivid green. Show faults: tabby markings.

Somali
Same as Abyssinian in two colors.

Red
Because of longer coat than Abyssinian, Somali appears lighter red.

Ruddy
Because of longer coat than Abyssinian, Somali appears more apricot.

Tonkinese
Although showing basic point-restricted pattern, depth of body color much darker hue than that of Siamese. Definite contrast between points and body color still apparent. Body shades to lighter cast on underparts in all five colors. Eyes vivid blue-green.

Blue Mink
Points deep slate-blue. Body soft blue-gray with occasional fawn overtones. Nose leather and paw pads same color as points, sometimes with a rosy cast.

Champagne Mink
Points medium brown. Body rich buff-cream. Nose leather and paw pads cinnamon-pink to cinnamon-brown.

Honey Mink
Points light to medium ruddy-brown. Body golden-cream with apricot cast. Nose leather and paw pads caramel-pink.

Natural Mink
Points dark brown. Body medium brown, often with ruddy highlights. Nose leather and paw pads point color.

Platinum Mink
Points pewter-gray with a lavender cast. Body very pale silvery gray. Nose leather and paw pads lavender to lavender-pink.

Cats and Owners

This list provides the names of all the cats photographed for this guide, along with the names of their owners.

1–4 Kittens
Owned respectively by Pamela Webster-Powell, Debra Dudley, Margaret Rice and Lynn Sherer, and Shirley Crawford

5 Tortie Point Himalayan
Monday's Call Girl
Owned by Joan Monday

6 Seal Point Himalayan
Cacao First Things First
Owned by Mike and Janet Altschul

7 Blue-Cream Point Himalayan
Jolee's Betty Boop
Owned by Ivan and Geri Raicevich

8 Blue Point Himalayan
Monday's Special Delivery
Owned by Joan Monday

9 Flame Point Himalayan
Klasikat's Straight from the Heart
Owned by Dick and Judy Mason

10 Shaded Cameo Persian
Anona Stardust
Owned by Harvey and Beverly Stobbe

11 Odd-eyed White Persian
Windborne Lalique of Klasikat
Owned by Dick and Judy Mason

12 Shaded Silver Persian
Sanskrit Twinkle
Owned by Joyce Hill

13 Van Calico Persian
Kashmur's How Sweet It Is!
Owned by Henry and Beverly Cain

14 Blue-Cream Persian
Seer's Molly May of Lotsafurr
Owned by Cherie Massaro and June Mourao

15 Red Persian
Jenita the Right Stuff of Camadine
Owned by Jerry and Marion Bodine

16 Red Classic Tabby Persian
Purr-Mor Play It Again of Petitpaws
Owned by Gloria Anderson

17 Tortoiseshell Persian
Pic-A-Bob's Bernadette
Owned by Dick and Judy Mason

18 Brown Classic Tabby Persian
Sarouk's Saar
Owned by William and Joan Benson

19 Black Persian
Eirewood's Elmer Fudd
Owned by Barbara and Roger Maxwell

20 Chocolate Kashmir
My Ty's Miss Mocha Fudge
Owned by Pat Romero

21 Tiffany
Sapphira Choclatrose of Sig-Tim-Hill
and Twinkie Choclatrose of Sig-Tim-Hill
Owned by Sigyn Lund

22 Brown Classic Tabby Norwegian Forest Cat
Mjavos Sangueetah
Owned by Susan Patrizzi

23 Seal Point Birman
Casa De Amor's Alberta Hope
Owned by Elizabeth Gemmell

24 Blue Point Birman
Casa De Amor's Alberta Blue Horizon
Owned by Elizabeth Gemmell

25 Brown Mackerel Tabby and White Maine Coon
McInkat's The Jazz Singer
Owned by Karen and Steve McInchak

26 Black Maine Coon
Calicoon's Jojoe
Owned by Margaret Rice and Lynn Sherer

27 Blue-Cream Maine Coon
Calicoon's Blu-Shadow
Owned by Margaret Rice and Lynn Sherer

28 Calico Maine Coon
Suzeran's Katie's Kelly
Owned by Sue Servies

29 Ruddy Somali
Rainkey's Starmoth
Owned by Brad and Sheila Bowers

30 Red Somali
Rainkey's Moondreams
Owned by Brad and Sheila Bowers

These same models appear in the charts, as well as in the black-and-white show poses for each breed account.

All photographs by Richard and Nancy Katris except for plates 21 and 22, by Alice Su.

---

31 Red Classic Tabby Cymric
Cathro Prince Cody Richard
Owned by Ron Cathro

32 Red Mackerel Tabby Cymric
Clacritter Rusty
Owned by Shauna O'Neil

33 Red-Lynx Point Javanese
Balimoor Sun Streak of D'Minium
Owned by Mary Minium

34 Seal-Lynx Point Javanese
McBali's Oreo
Owned by Fran McFarland

35 Lilac Point Balinese
Chesboro Moonshine
Owned by Gillian and Pete Melz

36 Chocolate Point Balinese
Picardy's Tahari
Owned by Anne Hodgdon

37 Mitted Seal Point Ragdoll
Ragnarok's Kong
Owned by Georgann and David Chambers

38 Blue Turkish Angora
Bereket's Maui of Duman
Owned by Debra Dudley

39 Black and White Turkish Angora Kitten
Owned by Debra Dudley

40 White Turkish Angora
Duman Esprit of Jeminai
Owned by Lee Brooke

41–44 Kittens
Owned respectively by Gay Turner, Susan Gollihugh, Cheri Wilkerson, and Susan Kidder

45 Red Abyssinian
Wil-O-Glen's Frankly Scarlett
Owned by Susan Kidder

46 Ruddy Abyssinian
Vanguard's Reveler
Owned by Carolyn Law

47 Blue Abyssinian
Tausert's Jameela of Tigress
Owned by Niki Haber

48 Russian Blue
Seenee Kat's Miklof
Owned by Thomas and Sydney Brosnan

49 Chartreux
Valley Video Ulanna
Owned by Alexis MacPherson

50 Bombay
Kats 'N' Klamms Bayberry of Fejuko
Owned by Frank Kovie

51 Burmese
Darina's Miss Muffet
Owned by Art and Marie Zeiner and Bob and Carole Salisbury

52 Blue Malayan
Tse-Mau's Lady Sings the Blues of Risu
Owned by Richard and Susan Mundell

53 Champagne Malayan
Anoka's Blonds Have More Fun of Temptations
Owned by Elizabeth Haydu

54 Platinum Malayan
Tse-Mau's Baby Doll of Risu
Owned by Richard and Susan Mundell

55 Blue Mink Tonkinese
Sonham's Sarah
Owned by Ann Sanson and Mary Masshammer

56 Natural Mink Tonkinese
Mangtai's Sugar Shack of Solano
Owned by Ann Sanson and Mary Masshammer

57 Seal Point Siamese
Cerissa Flashdancer
Owned by Cheri Wilkerson

58 Chocolate Point Siamese
Sea Shell's Suite Rhapsody
Owned by Nici Callahan

59 Lilac Point Siamese
Mr. Sweet Show Time of Sea Shell
Owned by Nici Callahan

60 Blue Point Siamese
Cerissa Rosanna
Owned by Cheri Wilkerson

61 Blue-Cream Point Colorpoint Shorthair
Lumax Whispurrs
Owned by Laura Bowman

62 Seal-Tortie Point Colorpoint Shorthair
Raksha's Kithan Killashandra
Owned by Laura Bowman

63 Seal-Lynx Point Colorpoint Shorthair
Lumax Symmetry
Owned by Laura Bowman

64 Red Point Colorpoint Shorthair
Ciara's Sunshine Superman of Lumax
Owned by Laura Bowman

65 Red Ticked Tabby Oriental Shorthair
Derry Down's Sunrise Surprise
Owned by Cherylee D. DeYoung

66 Chestnut Spotted Tabby Oriental Shorthair
Cerissa Sunspot
Owned by Cheri Wilkerson

67 Chestnut Smoke Oriental Shorthair
Beverlyhills Dustin of Cerissa
Owned by Cheri Wilkerson

68 Ebony Oriental Shorthair
Derry Down's Summer Nights
Owned by Cherylee D. DeYoung

69 Havana Brown
Debreaul's Duke Sir Dudley Too
Owned by Debbie Knable

70 Silver Egyptian Mau
Bastet's Princess Amira Silver Dots
Owned by Joyce McArthur

71 Blue Ocicat
Rolex's Gentle Blu Persuasion of Moontree
Owned by Cynthia Ives

72 Singapura
Changi's Minta
Owned by Hal and Tommy Meadows

73 Calico Cornish Rex
Gemdell Chatelain
Owned by Dell Sidney

74 Black and White Cornish Rex
Ripley's Sportin' Life of Nuffer
Owned by Jessica Newman and Susan Nuffer

75 Blue Mackerel Tabby Cornish Rex
Corydon Read 'Em and Weep
Owned by Mary Fellows

76 Red Classic Tabby Cornish Rex
Sophisticate Red Light Zone
Owned by Mary Fellows and Jacque Woodward

77 Tortoiseshell Devon Rex
Rexcentric Daisey Delite of Two to Win
Owned by Laurie Franklin

78 Cream Smoke Devon Rex
Rexcentric Susan Sox
Owned by Lesleyann Giles-Alpert

79 Brown Patched Mackerel Tabby and White American Wirehair
Thornwood's Ella Frizzgerald
Owned by Wayne and Shirley Field

80 Brown Patched Mackerel Tabby American Wirehair
Thornwood's Efrizzabeth Taylor
Owned by Wayne and Shirley Field

81 Silver Classic Tabby American Shorthair
Soledad's Sultan of Style
Owned by John Lanzendorf

82 Red Classic Tabby American Shorthair
Amex New Wave
Owned by Kathy Needham

83 Cameo Classic Tabby American Shorthair
Pantherpaws Pumpkin Patch
Owned by M. A. McCarthy

84 Cream Mackerel Tabby American Shorthair
Satin Song A. E. Newman
Owned by Ann Burke

85 Black Smoke American Shorthair
Soledad's Black Gold
Owned by Olen Wilford

86 Black British Shorthair
Anesa Merlin
Owned by Nora Wilson

87 Blue British Shorthair
Anesa Oliver
Owned by Nora Wilson

88 Blue-Cream British Shorthair
Welcome's Talley Ho of Jackats
Owned by Bill and Brenda Kinnunen

89 Blue and White British Shorthair
Excallibur's Boy George
Owned by Pamela Barrett

90 White British Shorthair
Top Fashion's The Crisco Kid of Jackats
Owned by Bill and Brenda Kinnunen

91 Chocolate Point Snowshoe
Twotowin's Si-Am Van-Turnip
Owned by Laurie Franklin

92 Korat
Jena Sawasdee of Si Sawat
Owned by Richard and Daphne Negus

93 Blue Exotic Shorthair
Lion House Bruno Bates
Owned by Susan Gollihugh

94 Blue-Cream Exotic Shorthair
Lion House Marvelous Mavis
Owned by Susan Gollihugh

95 Black Smoke Exotic Shorthair
Purrfun My Main Man
Owned by Lynn Brookhouser

96 Smoke Tortoiseshell Exotic Shorthair
Purrfun Trick or Treat
Owned by Lynn Brookhouser

97 White Exotic Shorthair
New Dawn Rainbo Chaser of Klasikat
Owned by Dick and Judy Mason

98 Red Classic Tabby Exotic Shorthair
Lion House Fearless Fredrick
Owned by Susan Gollihugh

99 Black and White Scottish Fold
Scottish My Earling
Owned by Lillian Johnson and Gay Turner

100 Brown Mackerel Tabby and White Scottish Fold
Scottish Redford
Owned by Gay Turner and Nancy Abbott

101 Red Mackerel Tabby and White Manx
Mariglen Suzanna of Merrimanx
Owned by Anna L. and Suzanne M. Sneiderwine

102 Red Classic Tabby Manx
Riagan's Rooney
Owned by Thomas Stahl

103 Brown Mackerel Tabby Manx
Bandera's Desperado of Merrimanx
Owned by Anna L. and Suzanne M. Sneiderwine

104 Black and White Manx
Glen Maye's All That Jazz
Owned by Gail Robinson

105 Black Manx
Glen Maye's Good Nuff
Owned by Gail Robinson

106 Sphynx
E.T.
Owned by William and Joan Benson

107 Mi-Ke Japanese Bobtail
Genji Tokyo Rose
Owned by D. Von Saxe-Coburg

108 Red and White Japanese Bobtail
Choneko Omoi of Vedalia
Owned by D. Von Saxe-Coburg

Cover
Singapura
Usaf's Rumah Muda and kitten
Owned by Hal and Tommy Meadows

Color Index

This index lists all the colors that are defined in the Color Glossary. Numbers in italics refer to pages.